The Primary Years

A Principal's Perspective on Raising
Happy Kids

Gail J Smith

First published by Busybird Publishing 2021

Copyright © 2021 Gail J Smith

ISBN
Print: 978-1-922465-51-1
Ebook: 978-1-922465-52-8

This work is copyright. Apart from any use permitted under the Copyright Act 1968, no part of this publication may be reproduced, stored in a retrieval system or transmitted in any form or by any means, electronic, mechanical, photocopying, recording or otherwise, without the prior written permission of Gail J Smith.

Cover Image: Kev Howlett
Cover design: Busybird Publishing
Layout and typesetting: Busybird Publishing
Illustrations: Kev Howlett

Busybird Publishing
2/118 Para Road
Montmorency, Victoria
Australia 3094
www.busybird.com.au

Acknowledgements

I thank all those families and staff with whom I had the privilege of working with over many years. The joy of working within a school community has been a major driver over the length of my career.

Also, my husband whose absolute support, drive and passion in encouraging me over the years has been an exceptional gift in my life. To my children, thank you for your continued encouragement, direction and belief in this project.

Welcome!!

The author suggests that after reading the introduction, you study the contents and find topics of interest, so that you can dip into the book at any time, as the need arises and find some guidance throughout the school term and year.

Contents

Introduction - Parenting in the Primary Years	1

PART 1 - Parenting Tips for Primary Years — 15

Chapter 1 - How you talk to your child is important — 17
- Body Language — 18
- Teach your child to recognise their gifts — 20
- Do we accept what parenting brings us — 23
- Watch the long explanations — 26
- What's in the words you use? — 29
- Always focus on the best parts — 32
- Take care with negative words — 34
- Incidental language — 36
- General language — 38
- Are you very opiniated in your views? — 41
- Timing is everything — 42
- Does your child know what you are saying? — 45
- It's okay to have an opinion — 47
- Giving Instructions. Who listens to that? — 49
- Understanding how your child processes — 52

Chapter 2 - Routine and structure — 55
- Routine leads to developing life habits — 56
- Structure in a child's life — 57
- What's wrong with a little downtime in our life? — 60
- Bedtime can be tricky — 62

Chapter 3 - Being a role model — 65
- Apologising is the key — 66
- Teaching children about themselves — 68
- Show confidence in your child — 70
- Being an effective listener and demonstrating justice — 72

Chapter 4 - Values — 74
- The value of problem solving — 75
- The value of helping others — 78

The value of being proactive	80
It's all about how we value children	84
Chapter 5 - How to influence your child's behaviour	85
Motivating children to change behaviour	86
Learn to be a coach, not an instructor	89
Don't linger on your child's behaviour	92
Parent's expectations and a child's place in the family	94
How do we build resilience in our children?	96
Children should see failure as a part of success	98
Setting goals	100
Confronting poor behaviour	102
What do we do when we don't like the behaviour?	104
Chapter 6 - Parenting	106
Who agrees with who in parenting?	107
Improvement and achievement – where do they begin and end?	109
What makes an effective parent?	111
Don't be a probing parent	113
Nine parenting tips to make life easier	116
Children learning about special national events	118
Chapter 7 - Enjoying the moment	121
Capture the moment and saviour the experience	122
Memories are lasting	124
Getting away from the maddening crowds	125
Chapter 8 - Being supportive	127
How to be helpful when a child is really upset	128
Giving real attention to your child	130
Chapter 9 - Strategies	133
Enjoying the process	134
Learning to deal with conflict	135
Asking for help	138
What time is the right time?	141
Short sharp breaks make all the difference	142
Teach our children to like themselves first	143
Keeping a happy journal that tells of success	145
Building a picture of success	146

A quick anger buster	147
Taking on something new	148
Developing independence early	151
Teach your child to develop staying power	154
Giving your child tools to defend themselves	156
Learning how to live without ownership of everything	157
Crazy and creative ideas for long stays at home	160

Chapter 10 - A child's brain	163
Is your child developing a growth mindset?	164
Do *you* have a fixed or growth mindset?	166
Does your child overthink?	168
Are you being a builder or a blamer?	170
Knowledge is Power	172
How to learn about patience	175
Teaching children the value of finishing	177
Judging people can have a powerful influence on our children	179

PART 2 - Families   183

Chapter 11 - Children and their families	185
The changing nature of families	186
Different generations	188
Some children need more attention	191
Being still and present	194

Chapter 12 - Teaching your children	196
Teaching cooperation	197
Letting the village teach your child	199

Chapter 13 - The home	204
Find conversation spaces	205
Creating space between yourself and your child	206
The importance of rituals in family life	208
Limits	209
How is the environment at home?	212

Chapter 14 - Learning from our children	214
Our children can teach us so much	215
Try being child-like	217

Chapter 15 - The bond between parent and child	220
The importance of keeping attachment strong	221
How important is it always to be the winner with your child?	223
The art of letting go	225
Always try to tell the truth	228
Chapter 16 - Siblings	232
It's just sibling business	233
When one child demands your attention how do the others cope?	235
The difference each child makes	238
Chapter 17 - Positivity	243
Celebrating the positive actions of others	244
Every day is different even for children	246
The art of being happy	247
A house of happy thoughts	249
Checking in on the happiness level of your family	250
Negative thoughts can get us down	253
Chapter 18 - Differences	256
We all have different ways of seeing he world	257
Teaching children about discrimination	258
Parents are different and that's okay	261

PART 3 - Helping Your Child with School — 265

Chapter 19 - The beginning	267
Pre-school experiences	268
Parents as early educators	270
Being supportive when starting school	271
Prep teacher – a child's perspective	272
Finding friends when you first start school	273
Ten easy ways to help children cope with early stress at school	274
Chapter 20 - Supporting your child at school	279
Children and school fatigue	280
Friendships are important	282
When things aren't smooth sailing	285
Tests	286
Make the most of your mistakes	288
Ten tips to support your child at school	290

Chapter 21 - Being in partnership with the school	292
School communication is the key	293
School grounds gossip	294
Confidentiality in a school setting	296
Chapter 22 - The school year	297
What's in a school year	298
Getting back to school after holidays	299
Who are your best friends at school? The office team of course!	300
Chapter 23 - Good habits	302
Keeping school attendance consistent	303
Simple tools to ease the stress of homework	305
Finding a balanced dose of media	306
Home is a great place to start reading	309

PART 4 - Anxiety — 311

Chapter 24 - The sources of anxiety	313
Be alert but not alarmed … the quiet child	314
Keeping an eye on the quiet child	315
Be alert to trauma in children	317
When separation occurs	319
Body image	322
Chapter 25 - Parents and their children's anxiety	324
Do we worry about our children becoming anxious	325
Feeling sorry is important – but within reason	328
Power games can be dangerous	330
How do *you* feel today?	333
Watch out for the doubting Thomas in your child	335
Chapter 26 - Practical ways to deal with anxiety	338
Weigh it up	339
Have you ever sat down and played with sand?	340
A picture is worth a thousand words	341
What an image can tell us	342
Lock it up and forget about it	343
It's only a balloon	344
For those that like a touch of drama	344
Reading through the problems	345

A little box with tricks inside	346
What number are you?	347
Chapter 27 - Strategies to manage anxiety	349
How to talk to children when they feel anxious	350
How to help your child cope	351
What's really the truth for a child?	353
The power of walking away	356
How to get rid of that blue feeling	358
Laughter a great tool in dealing with stress and anxiety	359
Afterword	363
About the Author	364
Index	365

Introduction

Parenting in the Primary Years

Over the years, and having worked in a range of settings which were demographically different, what have I learnt about the value of parenting in a child's life?

I've learnt that without the nurture and love from a parent or a significant guardian or carer, a child can be considerably disadvantaged. I'm not suggesting that a child's development will not be successful. However, from an early age, a child depends and needs the love and security of parents or guardians, which gives them the groundwork for feeling personally secure and comfortable with themselves.

Parenting over the years has changed, as society has changed. In the past, with bigger families, children developed more independence earlier. In today's world, smaller families and close parental involvement in a child's life has brought with it the challenge of children being more dependent for longer and less resilient in some cases. All societal changes come with their challenges and, of course, opportunities.

What I've observed is that if parents are effective listeners, give their children a chance to negotiate with them, put trust in their child as they show further independence and affirm their efforts and contributions, parenting is sound. When a parent allows their child to develop their own path but are there for support, their child starts to show independence and personal confidence grows.

There is a beautiful reflection by Kahlil Gibran in his book *The Prophet*. It sees the parent as a strong, unwavering bow and the child as the arrow. With the strength, clear direction and support of the bow, the child flies into the future with confidence and ease. The parent allows the child to fly ahead. They have worked hard to keep the bow strong and stable for the child to springboard into their own future. The bow's work is now done and the arrow flies into its own story.

Have you ever noticed how children who are living a balanced life appear busy and happy?

'Balanced' refers to having an active life in school and pursuits outside of school. Think about your own days at school. Did sport or other extra curricula activities give you a lift and a feeling of being fulfilled?

Children need balance and they learn through intellectual, physical, social and emotional means all intertwining and feeding off each other. Sports has always been a major factor in schools over the years. It was well understood centuries ago that it provided the physical boost that activates and refreshes our learning, not to mention its impact on building social stamina, teamwork and cooperation.

Having a balanced life allows a child to find appropriate breaks from formal learning. It also allows them to see success in different ways. Children who find studies difficult may succeed in sport. The more a child is exposed to a variety of ways to express themselves, the greater propensity they have to find areas of success. We know that success breeds success.

Over the years I've seen children finding success in different ways. If they felt more successful outside the classroom – perhaps through sport – this often fed into the classroom, as the child gained more personal confidence in their abilities, felt better valued by peers and so on.

Also, when parents provided balance to their child's life, the family coped better with many and varied issues. They seemed to be more open to looking at options and weren't rigid when it came to negotiations about school matters. We could call this developing emotional maturity within the family and this comes from providing a balanced and reasonable lifestyle.

I can't complete this introduction without mentioning the absolute value and power in reading and writing. Call a primary school what you like, but there is an expectation that the child will leave the school literate and numerate. These are key dimensions of any primary education and are the fuel for further learning.

No matter how we teach literacy and numeracy, the point is that it's taught and taught well. Over the years, the pedagogy shifts and there are different approaches to teaching literacy and numeracy; I'm not putting any value on one method more than another, instead it's all about the quality of teaching that makes the difference. It's relevant to add here that without parental support, literacy takes longer to acquire. When the learning of literacy and numeracy is seen as a whole effort by school and home, the child acquires the skills earlier, which benefits them by building their self-confidence and stimulates their interests in broader learning.

Everyone in the child's life must be encouraging and supportive of the learning of literacy and numeracy. This can be as simple as reading books at home, playing games, singing songs about numbers, counting chairs and so on. Children, through the stimulus of school and home, will build their knowledge and grow to love the journey of learning to read, write and to be numerate.

Finally, the influences on a child's development are innumerable. The environment, heredity, family life, nutrition, traumas are but a few factors that impact on a child's learning. What the relevant factor here is that the child, through all their learning experiences, grows to feel secure and happy within themselves. In my experience, this has always been the case. A child who feels that they are valued is more inclined to explore the world in challenging ways; they take risks and develop strong, confident personalities.

Every child will have a different journey, but if they feel supported and secure in themselves, they are more inclined to take up challenges, trust those around them and find many opportunities to learn where possible.

There's no question about it, the bow that flies the arrow sets the climate in which the arrow will go forward.

My experience in the school setting

Families constantly change and there are many shifting influences in the school setting.

After twenty-nine years as school principal and an earlier decade teaching, I've formed some strong beliefs about the journey taken by families through schools in the primary years.

These beliefs stem from reflecting on how a family journeys through the school system over many years. If there is one child in the family, their journey can be seven years. However, larger families may stay in a school setting for possibly ten to fifteen years subject to the size and spread of the family.

What a privilege it has been to journey with so many families. I saw families from their infancy stages of nervously leading their first child into school, through to their last child graduating. Watching the confidence of parents grow, and to see how they come to accept their children as they develop in all sorts of surprisingly different ways, has been a great joy for me.

What I've witnessed is the amazing growth and changes that occur in a family over time. When a change is profound, often the family grows in a whole new direction. A family is such an organic space. Here change, growth, experiences – good and bad – all influence the shape of that precious space in which a child is moulded and crafted into a young adolescent and later adult.

The relationship with the school is therefore very important, as the school plays such a significant part in that journey with a family through all its joys and crises. It's not just about providing a curriculum of learning for the child; it's about total education and support for the family. Children weave their way through all the challenges present in the school and home, as they themselves grow into young adolescents; the school is undeniably a strong catalyst in a child's development.

Once there are changes in the family, schools are sensitive to how this will impact a child.

The more the parents engage with the school and feel they're in a trusted situation, the better the child copes and stays connected to the school. This creates a stable environment and safe space for them.

Schools should be seen as a safe haven for children and families. It's an environment that is predictable, consistent and reliable; these are qualities important for the child and family to know and experience. As each new sibling begins school, the journey for the family shifts a little. The school is further enriched. Families should be actively engaged with the school to ensure that both parties are in a strong and comfortable relationship.

When parents connect to the school and put their trust and energy into the life of the school community, children benefit immensely. Children see harmony between their family and school. They see how parents commit to what is such an important and valued part of their life. Children also feel more at home in their school environment when they see families volunteering and being part of school life in different ways. Parents who become an active part of the life of the school also feel happier, as they have more intimate knowledge of school organisation, structure and the staff. They're not mystified or intimidated by the school, or subject to becoming anxious when negative whispers are around; they're comfortable in approaching the school at any time.

It was evident as a principal for many years, that families who saw the school as an extension to their family life, had a wonderfully enriching journey with the school and built strong relationships with other families, often lifelong. They took pride in their contributions which also enriched the school. Their children were comforted by their presence, saw excellent modelling from their parents and felt a strong interconnection and trust between home and school. There are many ways of being connected to the school and working parents are given varied opportunities to join committees or other types of involvement that impact on the overall life of the school.

I also reflect on the immense changes in education I've experienced over the years. These changes were greatly influenced by political movements which could, from time-to-time, unsettle school staff with changes of curriculum or new Government policies. Did it make considerable difference to a child's capacity to learn?

Well, it certainly influenced how we taught, but if the teaching was strong and well planned, shifts and changes in curriculum over the years made little difference to the final outcome of a child learning successfully. It was always about the capabilities of the teacher in ensuring that children were given optimum opportunities to learn. The burden of change did, however, fall heavily on schools and staff which occasionally created low morale given the amount of extra professional development required overtime.

We could say that as society was changing, how we taught changed and this influenced what was taught in the curriculum.

As educationalists, we have had to frequently change. We have bemoaned 'the good old days', gone through stages of affirming the changes, checking test results to guarantee that growth has occurred and so the list of verifying our work continues into the future.

Is there any one way in which a child will learn better, faster or smarter? I would argue not necessarily. Their capacity to learn isn't so greatly influenced by the style of curriculum presented. It's more connected to their interest in learning and the passion they have picked up for learning itself. Once a child discovers that they're capable learners and feel successful, they begin a learning journey of success, guided by good quality teaching and family support.

I sometimes reflect on the students of the eighties and nineties compared to those of today. I think about how successful they now are as adults well into midlife. What was different about their outcomes compared to today? I constantly come up with the same conclusion. With a supportive environment and capable teaching, all success is possible, no matter what the era is. This tells me that once parents have established themselves with their schools, all opportunities present themselves for the child when everyone is cooperating and celebrating the child's life together.

I've mentioned the importance of the teacher in the learning process. Over the years I've worked very closely with a myriad of teachers. Of course, you would expect difference in each teacher and, regardless of era, I'm thankful that teachers bring themselves and their unique style to teaching. Their role in influencing a child's capacity to learn is crucial. The longer I was in education, the more convinced I became about how unique and privileged the role of the teacher was. I also became aware, as we entered the more contemporary years, of how critical society had become about teaching. I noticed that compliance for teachers – changing laws on child safety and so on – impacted on a teacher's sense of well-being and confidence. Societal demands and an over demanding accountability on teachers influenced their confidence and ultimately their effectiveness.

This critique of teachers flows onto children and we must instead focus on having a trusting relationship between family and teacher. My experience clearly tells me that by connecting to your child's teacher in a positive way, this will greatly influence how secure they feel teaching your child. When problems occur, if you trust the teacher, you work on solutions together. Teachers take more risks and are happier in themselves when they feel valued and appreciated by parents and all of this flows into your child's performance. If trust and feelings of being recognised for their work is present, children are given optimum chances to succeed.

Across the decades, I was always looking to discover what a major catalyst was in a child being successful. It always came down to self-esteem. We have called it many names over the years: self-awareness, personal worth and so on. Over time we've also reflected on how best to build self-esteem and this has prompted much research into the matter.

Currently, we live in an era where there is a lot of discussion about children's resilience, their level of independence and their sense of self-worth and personal safety. In today's world, there is emphasis on their self-development. Our families are smaller and so the family operates differently than it did twenty years ago; parents have a more intimate relationship with their children. This, I believe, has had an impact on how children see themselves and how they operate in social settings. Their ability to be resilient is often regulated by the social climate in which we now live.

Having said this, what's important is how a child feels about themselves and this has a major influence on their success. I also believe that once a child learns that they're capable of success, they continue to build on that and are more inclined to take risks and learn in challenging ways. This principle was always the case in my experience both as teacher and principal. I also learnt that being successful came down to the opportunities offered in all of the various settings occupied by a child. This includes not just school but home, play and broader family experiences. Once a child internalises that they're capable and successful, they springboard into more opportunities of learning.

There is also no doubt that encouragement along the way is important, but not exclusively responsible for a child's feeling of success. Emotional maturity, as it develops, has a very significant influence on a child's perception of success in their world.

Do you ever stop and reflect on the images that influenced your thinking as you were growing up? An important aspect of a child's development can be the powerful images that they carry with them all their life. I remember holding my mother's hand, walking along a grey coloured wall on the first day of school and it was rendered very roughly. It was, what seemed to me, a very long, never-ending outside wall of the school. I touched it and I felt the rough edge of the concrete across the small, soft palm of my hand. In my mind I thought this was going to be school. Painful!

Images that a child experiences can be influential and lasting. Over the years I've been aware that children hold onto images.

Some are very pleasant, and others carry some negative memories that can rise to the surface. I was always aware that children may cling onto memories that can influence decisions they make along their journey of growing up. This isn't to say that negative memories are always damaging but, nonetheless, they do have an impression on a child and can play a part in influencing them.

Hence, what I've learnt is that if a child is exposed to plenty of positive experiences this makes them feel secure and happy and this is key, even though they do have memories of other images.

Think about your own childhood. What immediately comes to mind. Do you have positive images that influenced you? I'm sure there will be teachers that had an impact on you. Perhaps teachers who also impacted on you in terms of behaviours and attitudes *not* to be valued.

Sometimes important events can have memorable and lasting influences. It was also evident that powerful images can influence how a child processes, particularly in relation to their social and emotional development. It's important to provide a climate for children that is balanced and negotiable: a climate that comes with all its ups and downs but through discussion and ongoing honesty, children come to understand the world they live in with depth, sensitivity and empathy. This climate is owned by them and they are influential in its direction.

Have you ever thought about growth curves? These are times when a child demonstrates a leap of learning in some field. These can be legitimately seen – especially in a classroom – and are an opportunity for the teacher and/or parents to affirm and motivate a child in what was evident in their growth.

It's not uncommon to hear teachers comment on how a child has changed over the school holidays. Sometimes a change of scenery, new experiences, different ways to engage in activities can stimulate that growth spurt intellectually, physically, emotionally or socially.

These noticeable steppingstones in a child's development are worthy of applauding and recognising that growth occurs in different ways, not just in a classroom setting across a week, a term and a school year.

There are many factors that bring on these wonderful bursts of learning and self-confidence. I was always keen to observe the children as they showed new horizons across their learning journey.

The next part of this book is all about parenting and how it influences a child's learning across their primary years.

PART 1

Parenting Tips for Primary Years

Chapter 1

How you talk to your child is important

Body language

Are you an expressive person? Do your feelings show on your face or in the way you gesture? Many of us can be quite expressive and many keep a low profile when it comes to revealing all through body language.

For children it's all about reading their parents in different ways. Often this doesn't come from words, but from how a parent expresses themselves. A child is very skilled from an early age at reading their parent's body language. They're keen to know your reaction to their behaviour or simply to understand what you like or dislike.

Consider a baby in a crib. We smile at them to indicate pleasure and when a young child breaks a glass, we express displeasure through our expressions and words. There's no escaping the fact that how you express yourself is a tell-tale story to your child.

Consider that your body language can have a major impact on your child and should be used for good and not so much for expressing anger or disappointment. Positive, affirming body language will give reassuring messages to your child thus giving them an indication of how happy you're feeling. Eye contact is also very important as this demonstrates to your child that your focus is specifically on them.

Here are some reflections on how to use effective body language:

- When talking to your child, try to face them. If you're talking to a small child, come down to their level. This takes away a child's feeling that you're superior and indicates that you want to give them your attention.

- If you have something important to talk about, position yourself comfortably where you can give your child eye contact and you're directly facing them. This tells your child that they alone are important in this conversation and listening to them will be intentional.

- If you are trying to do several things at once – such as doing the dishes, watching television – while talking to your child, keep in mind that the conversation should be on a superficial level. Don't expect a great response!

- Watch the tone of your voice, much is revealed by this. Keep your tone the same as normal as changing tone can only unsettle a child who is always mentally checking in to see if all is well.

- Body language should be consistent when discussing anything. If you suddenly change body language – such as putting hands on hips, looking cross and frustrated – this will translate a message to your child. Remember that positive responses come from conversations where there is no subtle threat or subliminal power used.

- If you feel that you're in a state where your body language will dominate the conversation, consider waiting for a better time to talk.
- Smiling is a wonderful statement to make to your child. It says so much and tells your child that you're pleased and satisfied with everything.
- Using your eyes to express joy is also a positive act. How many people do we know that show a positive, inviting disposition through eye gestures, smiles and grins? They actually make us feel better.

We're always expressing ourselves to our children. Teachers are very sensitive to how they use body language when engaging with children. Consider how you use body language to reassure them of your feelings and to invite them into a warm and loving relationship.

> *'Your body communicates as well as your mouth. Don't contradict yourself.'*
> **– Allen Ruddock**

Teach your child to recognise their gifts

Do you know your strengths and unique capabilities? My guess is that you have a reasonably broad understanding and are quite comfortable with some of your qualities, but we can all be a little frayed at the edges when it comes to announcing our significant strengths. This is the same with children. Often, a child's slowly evolving self-confidence can give them doubts about their capabilities.

It's therefore necessary to articulate them loud and clear to your child. The sooner they recognise their strengths in themselves, the sooner they regularly begin to use them to their natural advantage. Once recognised and reinforced over and over again, the greater chance they retain it.

One obvious area in which most parents talk to their children about strengths is sport. Perhaps they're excellent runners or skilled in swimming. Sport is an area where parents feel very comfortable in supporting and recognising their children's capabilities. It's a comfortable and easy area in which to discuss a child's strengths.

What we're not so good at is articulating emotional strengths or general life strengths. We often neglect to recognise them as capabilities that need to be acknowledged. For example, perhaps your child is very compassionate to others or perhaps they're quick to resolve crisis amongst other children. Notice, for example, how effective your child is at calming someone who is unwell. They may be exceptional listeners. Is your child displaying a lot of self-discipline? Perhaps they should be congratulated for their organisational skills.

All of the above is about developing important life skills. By recognising them and talking to your child about them as capabilities, your child will come to identify them as valuable tools to use in life. For example:

> *'I've noticed that you're such a tidy person. You like order and this is one of your great gifts.'*

The child now knows that being tidy is recognised as a strength and should be valued. Before articulating this, the child may just see tidiness as a habit.

You can start affirming and articulating these strengths from an early age. For example:

> *'I love the way you play with other children.
> You're so fair and share all the time.'*

What a positive act it is to develop fairness and compassion at an early age.

When working with children, I was always conscious to remind myself of the gifts and capabilities of the child I was working with. They may have been great at sport or noted for their sense of humour. It was my goal to keep their strengths in mind when talking to them. Sometimes I could use their strengths to reinforce our conversation together. Teachers would frequently acknowledge children's strengths in the classroom. The more they reinforced their strengths, the deeper the awareness grew for the child.

As a parent, consider the following tips in ensuring frequent reference to your child's strengths:

- At mealtime, talk about gifts or strengths that you've noticed in your child that day. Sometimes just writing a note to them and leaving it in their bedroom is a wonderful spontaneous reminder. For example:

> *'What a gentle person you are. Today I saw how
> caring you were to your sister.'*

- When driving together, talk to your child about how you admire their gifts. List them and remind them of special strengths that you've noticed.

- Discuss people that your child knows who visibly demonstrate similar strengths. What do they like about them?
- If there are two parents living in the family home, talking about your partner's strengths and what attracted you to them is an excellent way to discuss the impact of such things in life.

We need to talk specifically about our child's very evident capabilities. Naming and labelling these strengths are a common tool used by teachers which helps to condition children into recognising them as important valuable life skills.

> *'Education begins the moment we see children as innately wise and capable beings. Only then can we play along in their world.'*
> **– Vincent Gowman**

Do we accept what parenting brings us?

Do we all want perfect children? I'm not quite sure what 'perfect' even is. In fact, I would question any parent who says that parenting is an easy ride.

Life isn't like that and children naturally want to grow and develop in ways that at times cause us some tension and stretch our imagination. Children are growing up in a different world to their parents and are being exposed to many and varied differences, not the least of which is technology driven.

As a first-time parent, we have expectations that we will be the best parent we can possibly be. In answer to this, I would say that you probably are, but the unknown is how your child grows and how they manage challenges in their world. How will they challenge us? How do we meet those challenges head on or gradually work with them in consultative ways? These are the big questions.

When working with families, it wasn't uncommon to hear parents talk about the unacceptable challenges that were put in front of them. They had no expectations that parenting would challenge their values, their thinking, put them in uncomfortable positions and, more importantly, force them to operate in ways that they thought impossible. Their whole world could be turned on its head by children's behaviour and attitudes to life. Parents can also look around and find that parenting for others seems easier.

Here I would say: what a wonderful challenge for you, as a parent, to be given the opportunity to think differently and to work closely with your child through their shifting world! Parenting should change and adapt to the growing needs of the child. It's not static and will demand you reflect on your values and ideas and at least consider different ways of looking at life.

Teachers can see the fatigue of parents in trying to understand their child's behaviour or school performance. As a principal, it wasn't uncommon to support teachers in their supporting of parents struggling with their child's lack of achievements.

The question I pose here is whether, as a parent, we become unhappy when the child's behaviour isn't what we expect.

Are we expecting standards that suit us? Are we wanting them to operate like us?

Here are some thoughts on how to accept that parenting will surprise us and ultimately delight us:

- Take care to enjoy the differences you notice in your child. Often, we look for the similarities in our children and reward them. For example:

    'I was good at maths and so I expect you to be as well.'

- Be prepared to be surprised. This should be a regular feeling. Enjoy the moment and comment on the surprise. For example:

    'Wow. I'm so impressed that you choose such different colours to wear out.'

- Talk about how you love the differences that you notice in your child. This gives them a feeling that they can express themselves comfortably around you.
- As a family, talk about how everyone is different and how those differences make a wonderful family tapestry, woven with unique story and experiences.
- If there are behaviours that you don't like and have reason to talk about them, do it in such a way that you're not stifling their right to see things differently.

- For example:

> *'I would like to talk about those clothes you're choosing to wear to the beach; I do have some concerns about their suitability. Perhaps let's start by telling me why you think they're suitable.'*

Here you're not condemning their ideas, in fact you're demonstrating an interest in listening to their reasoning. Even if, after negotiation, you child needs to change their clothes, affirm the fact that they're developing their own style and that this is a good thing. Include at least one aspect of their dress choice to show you value their opinion. Perhaps you could go shopping to learn more about what they like.

If your child realises that you value their opinions, they're less likely to be reactive to your opinions and values.

Accept what parenting brings. It will take you on an amazing voyage where you'll discover in yourself different and unexpected ways to grow. Imagine that! You too will grow with your child.

> *'There are two things a parent should give a child. One is roots, the other is wings.'*
> **– Anonymous**

Watch the long explanations

Ever wondered what your time span is for listening to others? I imagine it would vary subject to the person, fatigue and interest in the topic. My point is that as we talk to people, the longer the sentence and overall conversation, the greater the propensity for our attention span to drop off. Now think about our children. They're not as well developed as adults in concentration and the younger the child, the more limited they are in hearing everything you have to say.

It's also well known that if your child is anxious or feels distracted, the likelihood of them hearing everything you said will deteriorate very quickly. If there is an important message you wish to give a child, especially a pre-schooler, it's worth asking them to repeat it back so that you understand if they took in the key message.

Our tone of voice can also impact how much a child hears and processes. The more aggressive we sound, the more the child will shut down and only hear the hostility.

It's also true that if we give long explanations to children, no matter how informative the information, they will process in chunks of information and they may not get the full impact of what you're saying. In fact, it's possible that if the explanation is very long, they can chunk concepts together which make their understanding completely incorrect. Teachers are very aware of how children process information and will limit the sentences to suit the situation.

When we want to give an explanation to a child, we should consider their age, attention span, wellness, timing and interest in concentrating at the time. If a child has plenty of distractions around them, they won't find it easy to concentrate on the explanation.

I recommend that you choose your time wisely. Then consider what the actual information is that you want to give your child and construct your sentences clearly while keeping them short.

When working with children, despite having considerable experience in this field, I would still regularly check myself and reflect on what I wanted to say. It was important to be succinct and clear. Using vocabulary that suited the age of the child was most important. When I gave long explanations to children, it wasn't uncommon that they would respond saying, 'I don't know what that means?' This was a clear message that they had lost the content of what I was saying.

Consider the following as tools to help talk to children in ways that will engage them and give you the best response:

- Think before you speak. Is it important at that time to discuss the matter or can it wait for a time where the child will be more receptive? Are you adequately prepared to give the best explanation?
- Choose words carefully and, if discussing an important matter, use vocabulary that is simple and direct.
- Short, sharp sentences are the best to get your message across to your child.
- Wait for a response rather than charging in quickly. Children need that time to process what you've said. A little silence in between talking is quite acceptable.
- Have a positive tone to your voice that isn't loud or sharp. Children only hear the aggravation and not the words.
- Always acknowledge their listening. For example:

'Thanks for listening today. Now we can get on with dinner.'

- If you're uncertain that a child has understood what you said, gently ask them in a positive and encouraging way to repeat what you said. For example:

  'Can you just tell me what I said?'

- When you wait for a response be positive, as negative body language can shut down a child's response and limit their comprehension of what you had to say.

'The way we talk to our children becomes their inner voice.'
— **Peggy O'Mara**

What's in the words you use?

The power of words has such an impact on our children. Think about words used by your family when you were a child. Perhaps they were reinforcing or damaging. Either way, words are powerful tools in influencing our self-image. How we express ourselves reveals a lot about who we are to others and especially to our children.

This doesn't mean that parents should be wordsmiths, but it does suggest that what we say to our children and how we deliver the message needs to be thought through carefully. Consider the following statements:

'Clean the table, it's full of leftover dishes.'

> *'I would appreciate you cleaning the table because it will really help me.'*

> *'I love a clean table. Thanks for your help. Let's clean it up.'*

Ultimately, the goal is to clean the table, but how we express this requires clear messages to your child and highlights your mood, temperament and how you desire to engage with your child.

Also consider your choice of words. For example:

> *'That's a stupid thing to do.'*

When talking to children, they will always look for intent and seek clarity in what you say. Given that they seek approval from you, they need to have conversations with you that are not destructive or display irrationality. Of course, when you need to discuss and deal with unacceptable behaviour, you'll need to speak to them with assurance and firmness, but I recommend the following:

- Say what you need to say and no more. Sometimes in our anxiety to deal with the matter, other issues are brought into the conversation which can blur the whole purpose of the conversation.
- If you think that you won't handle the conversation well, then delay the timing of the discussion.

- Remember that when a child is anxious, they often don't hear or process the whole conversation. Use gentle words that are clear to your child. For example:

    'I want to talk to you about the broken glass on the floor. It seems that you knocked over the vase when you were running. Do you remember our discussion about running around the room?'

- Take care not to use language such as 'stupid', 'dumb' or 'silly'. Often, a child focuses on these words which cloud their feelings of self-worth when you're talking to them.
- On a positive note, when you affirm a child use language that is recognisable and valued by them. Use familiar, comforting words in which they can identify. For example:

    'I'm so impressed with your efforts. Well done.'

The words we use and how we phrase our words dictates to many people how we interpret the world. Your child sees you as a major role model in their life and will mimic your style as they get older. In the classroom, it was quite common to see children who sounded so much like their parents. Never underestimate how your language influences your child.

'You can speak well if your tongue can deliver the message of your heart.'
– John Ford

Always focus on the best parts

As I have just outlined, language and how we use it can be a tricky process. It can be the vehicle for success in building relationships as well as being a destructive tool when used inappropriately. We often say one thing but mean another. Children are very quick to pick up on the negative of anything we say about them. Sometimes we refer to them in conversation casually and we may be subtly mentioning their inadequacies in some way, yet unaware of the damage caused.

It's amazing how in a school setting a child will quickly pick up on any aspect of a teacher's conversation that referred to them or especially to their poor performance. They are quick to personalise statements that we make as they seek out our support and, most importantly, look for how much they are valued in our eyes.

It was quite common for a child who felt devalued to lose interest, not perform or react with poor behaviour. It sometimes took considerable time to establish what the problem was, and it often came down to a personal statement made by the teacher which they interpreted for themselves as negative.

We have the ear and heart of our children. We're very visible to them and they are very sensitised to how and what we say, especially when it affects them.

Here are a few ideas on how to talk about the best of your child wherever possible:

- If you have nothing positive to say at the time, say nothing. Silence is golden when you're not sure what to say. It causes no harm and gives you time to rethink the situation.

- Notice the little things that you can comment on throughout the day:

    'Well done, you know how to set a table.'

    'Great effort on starting your homework.'

    'Bravo for cleaning the table so well.'

    'You're very fast at picking up the Lego blocks.'

    'I always like your smile; it makes me feel good.'

- Notice that these quick conversations are small ego boosters and reassure your child that they're valued and have achieved well in your eyes.
- If you need to talk about other matters such as poor behaviour, remember to end on a positive note. For example:

    'I'm sorry that you shouted at your brother. You're usually such a gentle person.'

- Note that you're reminding your child that you look for the positive aspect of them but recognise that they make mistakes which must be addressed.

- When talking to others and referring to your child build in some positive talk.

- Talking about the best of your child brings the best out in them. They enjoy hearing you talk about what you enjoy about them and, the more public you are, the more you give voice to their valued character.

- When a child needs discipline and behaviour is unacceptable, this is a time for active listening to establish what has led to the behaviour. This should be followed with some consequences through negotiation and discussion. It should, however, end with giving your child those words of reassurance that highlight how much you value them and trust in their character.

Talking about the best in your child is intermittently building the foundation blocks of a strong relationship with your child. It gives them reassurance.

Take care with negative words

Sometimes words stick! Especially if they're offensive.
As the old saying goes:

> *'Sticks and stones will break my bones,*
> *but words shall never hurt me.'*

Totally untrue! I would say that most issues on the schoolyard that ended in fights were caused by the use of inappropriate words, mostly name calling.

In my experience, angry, upset children who were cross with their parents, teachers or friends would talk about the words that were used against them. For example:

'Don't be silly. The answer is in the book.'

'You play footy like a monkey.'

Now, in each of the above statements the person speaking would naturally deny that they called a child a name. Actually, all the child heard was the name and that made them feel very uncomfortable and hurt. They quickly identified with the name. For example:

*'That was a silly thing to do.
The lid was clearly on the bench.'*

All the child hears is that they were called 'silly' while the person making the statement would say that they referred to the act of being silly and not the person. Too late! All that is heard and interpreted is the word 'silly'.

Teachers often find themselves in a dilemma with students if they slip in their use of such words. They take care not to use words like 'silly', 'dumb', 'stupid' and so on, as the child takes on the message that it refers to them.

Here are some common words we often use in our language: 'silly', 'dumb', 'stupid', 'ugly', 'ridiculous', 'lazy', 'careless', 'selfish', 'ignorant'. I've heard children complaining about all of these. They're words which children internalise and consequently feel upset by. Once the word is heard, the rest of what is said falls short. It's best to take the safest route with children and avoid such words in your conversations no matter in what context you were using them.

> *'Sticks and stones may break my bones, but words will definitely hurt me!'*

Incidental language

One of the most powerful ways we influence our children is the language we use with them. We may do many things for our children but how we use our language is critical in how they understand our intent and how they recognise their role.

How we speak incidentally has a big impact on our children. Sometimes during a conversation with our children, we can incidentally make a negative statement about them. It comes as no surprise when we get a negative response. For example:

> *'John, let me carry that over to the bench. It's too heavy for you.'*

> *'Do your homework in that room, it's a silly thing to do it near the television.'*

In both these statements we refer to their level of competency. It's better to say something like:

> *'John, I'll carry that over to the bench, but thanks for your help,'*

or

> *'You can do your homework in a room where there is less noise'*

It's necessary to get your message across but take care that the language you use is deliberate and considered. We can do this very effectively without being aware of its destructiveness or the regularity with which we say it.

We can develop patterns in our talk where a child's vulnerable side is mentioned quite often. For example:

> *'You're not big enough to help mum. You can help when you're older.'*

This way of speaking can become a habit and can spread to other members of the family who pick up the intent and run with it themselves. Sometimes the order of the family can be a factor here.

When working with children, they would mention the perception that the family had of them at home. This would affect their own self-perception and, in some cases, how they acted out with others. For example:

> *'Jenny, you know how clumsy you are, be careful when you carry that plate!'*

Instead, try saying:

> *'Jenny, thanks for taking the plate. Take care.'*

The outcome here is likely to be more successful or at least there is no incidental labelling.

It's all in the words.

> *'People may hear your words, but they feel your attitude.'*
> **– John C Maxwell**

General language

Be careful with the general language you use around children. The minute we start talking we reveal a lot about ourselves. The intonation of our speech and the expressions we use are learned habits and, no surprises, become learned habits for your children.

We can use language to build relationships with our children, ward off problems and act proactively when communicating around and with our children.

As a principal, modelling effective language was an important statement to a child. Being consistent and authentic in how and what I said was critical to maintaining a successful relationship with all members of the school community.

Firstly, it's helpful to recognise that our moods and general health will affect how we communicate. The best advice I can give is to always do less, talk less and slow down, using less communication if you're feeling vulnerable in discussing matters. This is acting proactively and reducing dialogue that can be damaging.

The following are suggestions to assist in providing effective language when around children:

- Remember to use your child's name when talking to them and avoiding using 'you' and other nicknames that are not considered endearing.
- When talking, take care to slow down, especially when taking about something important. Talking too fast sets up a feeling of anxiety and a need for an immediate response.
- Try to build in positive, reassuring language. For example:

> *'I love that happy face when we clean your room.'*

> *'Television is finished and it's bedtime.*
> *Sleep is a great time to rest that body.'*

- Use the same tones when talking. A child will pick up very quickly when the tone changes. They will then try to interpret your attitude.
- Some families introduce new words once a week. They then practise using the word to include it in their speech.
- Another important behaviour is to carefully think through what you want to say, rather than correcting yourself. This helps children recognise the clarity in your conversation.
- When working with children, the rule is to always talk to them in your regular tone of voice when you're well prepared with what you need to say. This ensures that they don't get confused and you're in a better situation to talk with clarity and control.

There is nothing more frustrating than someone talking to you about an issue when they're confused, unclear, repetitive or unsettled about what they want to say.

- Sometimes talking in simple sentences with a small breathing space in between statements is helpful to children, as they're learning to process information.
- Watch the dramatics when talking. They can also be confusing for a child by providing inaccurate messages.
- Choosing good language phrased as positively as possible has the best chance of being received well. Roadblocks to a child come from language that is intimidating, loud and confusing.
- If you're inclined to talk calmly and in an even pace, this would apply to both child and adult. Remember that there is an emotional message in what you have to say. The child will always look for that hidden message.
- If a child responds to your conversation and they're completely not on target with what you had to say, this is a red-flag signal that they haven't actually heard you properly.

Our language is a powerful tool which can be used for good and bad. As a parent, we have such a rich opportunity in building strong, confident children, who use language as a force to get their message across in the most effective way possible. They learn this through how we distribute our messages.

> *'Each day of our lives we make deposits in the memory banks of our children.'*
> **– Charles R Swindoll**

Are you very opiniated in your views?

You might ask, *what has this to do with rearing our children?* Stop and think for a minute with regard to how you express your opinions. Children will quickly pick up if you have and demonstrate strong, loud opinions with little room for negotiation. Some people have a tendency to be quite vocal and passionate about their beliefs and opinions.

While I appreciate that the home is an environment to be yourself and express your opinions, I invite you to think about the set of little ears listening to your reactive behaviour to issues. Children who have parents with strong opinions will often respond by simply being quiet. This is a protective means of not getting caught up in crossfire and not challenging what appears to be a strong force in the house. A child learns early to keep their opinions and beliefs to themselves. This is a form of self-protection. The question I pose here is do we want our children to feel they can offer opinions that have value and can be considered in the family discussions?

Children who appear confused about this will go directly to other sources to express their opinion or seek advice from unreliable sources.

When working with children in the school setting, children would often comment on how satisfying it was to talk to their friends about issues, as their parents were too strong in their opinions. They enjoyed feeling heard and felt some empowerment in being listened to and having their beliefs approved. They believed that when they didn't understand something, they felt more comforted to talk to friends rather than getting the full entourage of opinion and attitude from parents.

A child's level of maturity will dictate how they interpret matters, but our job as parents is to understand their opinions and offer advice with an appreciation of their right to develop their own opinions. Children are more inclined to keep approaching their parents if they feel they have a voice that is valued and that will be understood and heard. You could say to your child:

> *'Thank you for your thoughts on that matter. It sounds like you've given it some thought.'*

A child will always want to go to the source of formative opinions, their parents, but the source must be one that listens and understands that a child's growing awareness needs guidance, appreciation and support.

> *'Don't let the noise of other's opinions drown out your inner voice.'*
> **– Steve Jobs**

Timing is everything

How often do we get timing right or wrong with our children?

It's amazing how dealing with issues at the right time can make such a difference with children. It also helps when, as the adult, you're approached in a good mood, as the discussion is more likely to be successful for all concerned.

Children are also prone to having better times and less suitable times to discuss important matters. Often, we mistake a 'no' response as meaning they don't know or care and this can completely miss the mark.

Sometimes in the rush of the day and in the moment, when we want solutions or answers, we press our children for a response. Sometimes this isn't forthcoming and can result in frustration all round. The beauty of choosing the most effective time means that you're more inclined to be successful in getting the best response. Think about yourself for a moment. When you're feeling unwell or your mind is on other things, you show less interest in being responsive to other people's questions and requests.

Here are some tips on how to use timing to your advantage:

- Consider how tired your child is at that time. Tired children listen with less interest.
- Is your child well enough to give you a suitable response?
- When asking an important question, consider the distractions present. Is your child focused on something else, perhaps watching their favourite television show? A preoccupied child isn't a great listener.
- Choose times when your child is relaxed and not too focused. Some parents find asking questions while driving together is an excellent time to get a response.
- Ask questions when you're feeling ready. If you're busy and loaded with emotional agendas this isn't

the best time for your child to give you what you need. They are quick to pick up your pace and will give you a safe response.

- When your child is happy, this is a good time to step into the realm of questioning. If they feel relaxed and happy, they're more responsive in their talk and feel less vulnerable.

- If your child is feeling pressured over different matters this isn't the best time to talk about extra issues, they can wait. A mentally overloaded child will simply shut down or demonstrate poor behaviour when it all gets too much.

- When considering when to ask tricky questions, ensure that you have built a positive framework or platform with your child. This may mean affirming them and acknowledging their contributions when you have a discussion.

- If you ask an important question and you get an unclear response, just remind yourself that for some reason your child isn't ready to respond. Perhaps you could say:

> *'It seems it's not the right time to talk about that at the moment. I'll chat with you later.'*

This also gives your child some preparation time in thinking about their response.

- If you have several issues to talk about with your child, only try talking about one issue first. Children process information quite differently using a different pace. Overloading questions all at once will give you no satisfaction with the response you receive.

- Remember not to become too frustrated if you choose a time and it doesn't work out. We're not mind readers and sometimes a child just needs some space, and we need to respect that fact.

When working with children at school, timing was everything. I knew when I had failed by the look and response of a child. It was necessary to respect all the various influences that came into the daily life of a child and measure the best time to engage in important conversation.

Does your child know what you're saying?

Some might just say it's all in the interpretation. Often, when we have conversations with our children, we naturally presume that they fully understand and grasp the concepts that are being discussed. Younger children, especially pre-schoolers, may only hear part of what you had to say as they will process some of the conversation but not necessarily all of the conversation.

Older children may still struggle to hear and process all of what you say. This will definitely be the case if you're angry or disappointed and talk to them in a frustrated tone.

When teachers talk to children about some concern they may have, they receive a better response when they speak slowly and only cover one or two concepts. Long protracted sentences won't be internalised by the child.

It was always necessary to carefully speak in simple and short sentences. For example:

> *'I would like to talk to you about ...'*

It's then that you can mention the issue, but only one or two facts at a time. For example:

> *'When the incident happened,*
> *you got very angry.'*

> *'When you were angry you ...'*

When you listen to what they say, take care not to then barrage them with too many details. Simply talk about the matter at hand.

When working through problems with children, it was common to first ensure that they were listening and not too anxious. Anxiety is an emotional blocker, and children will simply shut down.

The following tips can help when talking about issues with a child:

- Use shorter sentences to describe the issue.
- Remember to listen as soon as you have expressed your concern.
- Allow silence to happen between conversations with a child. This is their way of processing.
- Be empathetic to their listening skills understanding that, at first, they may not have interpreted your concerns.

- Repeating the concern is fine but it should be done gently and with no frustration in the voice.
- Remember that younger children will need simple sentences with easily understandable language.
- Don't use emotive language. For example, 'That was a foolish thing to do,' or 'You're crazy to clean the kitchen that way.' Children will focus on those negative words and often ignore the content of what you're saying.

A child can shut down in various ways. Some get angry and reactive; some go silent or some appear to ignore the conversation. When the shutdown occurs, check in that the child understood what you actually said, rather than becoming angry that they didn't respond. Becoming angry only escalates the issue of the child not hearing you.

I often heard these words from a child:

'I don't know what mum wants from me.'

Less words can often be more effective.

It's okay to have an opinion

Are you the sort of person that is overwhelmed when strong personalities talk over you? This can be frustrating. As we grow and develop on emotional, social, intellectual and physical levels we find our place in groups and especially in conversation with each other.

Some people become shy and timid while others develop more confidence in expressing themselves. Whatever the developing personality of your child, they need to find a space for their voice and the best place to start is in the comfort of the family.

They need ongoing and regular opportunities to be heard and have the time to express themselves. Some families have special listening times at dinner.

A child needs to know that they have a voice which is valued, and that people want to hear what they have to say. This is a right and if they develop feelings that they have opinions that are valued, their self-confidence grows. This is about strengthening their emotional maturity. They hear and listen to a conversation but recognise they can have opinions and offer comments in that conversation. They will always see their parents as role models in terms of how they communicate with different groups.

When working with children, after listening carefully to their concerns, it was quite common to include:

'So, what do you think about this?'

'Do you think there is value in that idea?'

Giving a child the right to a voice gives them the understanding that they are valued. It also teaches them the art of conversation and develops their listening skills and improves literacy skills. Here are some suggestions to give them a voice:

- At dinnertime, bring up a topic and ask each child to talk about their thoughts and opinions on the subject. Some parents use simple news items of the day.

- Ask your child to write down opinions on a topic. Put them into a box and, at dinner, read out everyone's opinions and discuss.

- When the family talks about an issue, write opinions on a post-it-note and put it on the fridge. This is an interesting way to later discuss the issue as a family.

- When watching a film together, stop along the way to ask opinions about something that has happened in the film. This sparks conversation.

We're helping our child grow in confidence to use their voice effectively and to feel reassured that their opinion is important. It may not be the overarching opinion of everyone, but it has a legitimate place in conversation.

'Education begins the moment we see children as innately wise. Only then can we play along in their world.'
– Vince Gowman

Giving instructions. Who listens to that?

I wonder how many instructions we give in a day as parents.

'Get dressed quickly.'

'Get into the car, we're going.'

'Put your clothes away now.'

'Don't do that, you're hurting your brother.'

No surprises that children's listening abilities drop, which causes so much frustration for busy parents.

Repeating instructions when there is no response from children becomes a trap as it can lead to the escalation of frustration for parents. There are various reasons why children stop listening, but it's primarily concerned with the number of directions that begin to fall on deaf ears. The pattern of repeating the questions forms part of the culture of the home. We may give directions that are poorly timed, repeated differently, are vague, escalate in volume or come with negative body language.

We can become upset that the child isn't responding and valuing what we say. Often, the child just hasn't internalised the message. Of course, with technology in the home, listening to a parent's request is further compromised.

And how often do we just threaten to take the technology away?

I would recommend the following strategies to ease the pain:

- Discuss at a restful family time what intructions you need to give in advance. Ask your child to repeat what the tasks are and, most importantly, give them a sound reason for doing the task. For example:

> *'You need to be quick in the morning when you get ready so I can get to work on time. Your help will make my day much better. Thanks.'*

Most importantly, when it works out well, remember to thank your child for supporting you. For example, a child may never see the value in cleaning their room because, for them, there is no problem. However, if you want the clean room, it's all about the difference it makes to you. Of course, not all instructions may have an impact on you, they may simply be about developing good habits. Tell your child that you both need to follow instructions because it will make an important difference. For example:

> *'Please get in the car quickly as traffic will build up behind us and it's safer.'*

A child will follow instructions and change behaviour if they see the value in doing so.

- Choose the best time to give instructions and be realistic with your expectations. If a child is preoccupied, you may need to reflect on when and how you give instructions. Also, think about how important the task is to you. Is now the best time to give instructions?
- Use positive body language and acknowledge when your child responds quickly. For example:

> *'Thanks, let's get this task done quickly so that we can have some time together.'*

- Negotiate where possible. For example:

> *'If you tidy your room quickly then we can have some time to play Lego together.'*

- When working with children in the school setting, I noticed one significant factor that encouraged a child to listen with intent and it involved using their name. For example:

    'Mark, could you open the door please?'

    'Anna, please pass that pencil to me.'

    'Josh, could you please close the door?'

The family environment is the setting in which you operate with your child most of the time. Keep in mind that your modelling of listening and responding to others is always in the watchful eye of your child. The more you create a climate of listening, positive feedback and keeping voices at a calm and steady level, the greater propensity there is to reduce the escalation of anger and frustration when giving instructions. These are the skills you're teaching your child; it's all about developing a culture of listeners.

Understanding how your child processes

Are you an open-ended person who enjoys doing activities that can have many optional ways of responding? This is about accepting the freedom to respond in various ways and embracing the big picture. Or are you more inclined to enjoy closed activities? Do you prefer to be more in control of everything with clear understandings of outcomes? Our children are no different. As they get older, they'll find that school will provide activities where they'll need to work on open-ended problems. Sometimes, teachers will give them closed exercises that will involve simple and clear answers.

Now apply this to your experience at home.

When you have tasks to do, reflect on whether you're setting open-ended tasks or more closed tasks with clear outcomes. Consider whether your child understands what's expected of them.

For example, would you ask your ten-year-old to tidy up the yard? This request is so broad, and this can lead to frustration. It's better to give explicit instructions about one aspect of the yard and what you expect done. Asking them to repeat the instructions back to you is also beneficial. This is a closed activity, and your child knows exactly the parameters of the request.

Children are keen for approval and sometimes they can't grasp the request so understanding your child's mode of thinking is very helpful as it reduces tension between you both. Also, praise your child for achieving the tasks because this increases the likelihood of more success.

Your child will begin to appreciate that how you talk to them is understandable, reasonable and possible to achieve and this helps them tune in to what you're saying. It's better to have an understanding of how they process so that damage to your relationship is reduced to a minimum.

Also, keep in mind how much information your child can process at once. This is especially applicable to younger children. It's all about how many instructions you give them at once.

For example:

> *'Go to the fridge, get out the milk and put it on the bench next to the cup.'*

There are four instructions in one sentence.

Some children may have only heard two instructions. No surprise that the milk ends up in the wrong area! If your child only processes two instructions, then give them only two instructions at once.

> *'Go the fridge, get out the milk. Thanks for that. Now put it on the bench, next to the cup. Well done for being helpful.'*

Notice that saying 'well done' is followed by a reason for the approval. Often, your child doesn't understand what made the activity worthy of praise. The message I give is to tune into how your child processes to further enrich your relationship.

Chapter 2

Routine and structure

Routine leads to developing life habits

Some people love routine and others struggle with keeping up the pace of routine. We're all different in managing our lifestyles. Whatever style you've adopted, remember that you're modelling patterns for your child. I'll now specifically discuss regular attendance at school.

This is a pattern worth developing. The more a child values being in school each day, the more they will understand routine. As a principal, it wasn't uncommon to see children unsettled returning into a classroom later in the day or after several days' absence. Of course, illness can interfere in regular attendance but attending school on time every day provides stability and predictability for a child. They love routine and feel secure in knowing how their day will start. They're conscious of relationships with their peers and understand how they can destabilise when they're not regularly present at school. They become sensitive about the relationships they've formed in the classroom and how prolonged absences can potentially change these relationships.

All families are busy and have different ways of operating; the size of the family, working parents, sick children and so on, all impact on how a family starts the day. Attempting to make a good start each day demonstrates to your child that it has priority in family life. Perhaps discussing as a family how this can best work and agreeing to morning routines may help.

Some parents set up a weekly chart and tick off their good habits each day in following morning routines. They even celebrate at the end of the week when the routine worked. Whatever the method, the message to the child is that regular and punctual school attendance is strongly valued.

Structure in a child's life

As just discussed, routine gives us predictability and reassurance. We grow familiar with routine and we can rely on its regularity. Having said this, I would be the first to say introduce variety and flexibility into a child's life. They need to create and explore outside the routine of everyday life. Being creative and stretching the imagination takes them into new territories of growth on so many levels. They also start to value being a risk taker.

Providing variability is important for a child's growth, but I'll now talk in defence of routine and structure.

A child needs periods of calm and stability in their life. They need predictability and this comes with putting in place some suitable structures and boundaries. When a child's world is turned upside down through, for example, family crisis, the first thing they often crave is routines and boundaries, as they are comforting and reassuring.

At the beginning of each school term, children love being back in the predictability of classroom routine. Here they can evaluate themselves and measure success more easily. There is a comfortable familiarity and measurability about the classroom.

When working with children who were having some anxiety issues, it was common practice to keep the environment in which we chatted consistent. It was also important that I maintained my usual predictable tones and worked in a familiar way with the child. These structures acted as a safe and predictable boundary in which to engage. The minute I stepped out of these boundaries, the child would become confused and struggle in responding to me comfortably.

Here are a few thoughts on putting boundaries and structures in place:

- Ensure the boundary is realistic and that your child understands the purpose of the boundary.
- Set up weekly routines at home with regard to basic issues such as homework routines, reading in bed, eating between meals and so on. These can be discussed regularly with the family and renegotiated where necessary.
- Where possible, invite your child into setting up routines for themselves. It's always much more likely to be successful if it comes from your child. For example:

*'What time do you think is reasonable for bed?
Let's discuss the jobs you have to do before bed
to work out bedtime.'*

- Discuss some routines you have set up for yourself. Talk about why the routine helps you in different ways.
- Talk about the structures that are set up in the classroom. This is an excellent way of talking about the value of structures. For example:

*'So, your teacher lets you eat snacks ten minutes
before the bell. Why does she do this?'*

- Pets are an excellent opportunity for a child to develop important structures that impacts on a pet's quality of life.
- If you're planning a holiday, discuss with your child some structural issues that need to be considered.

*'We're going camping soon, let's make a list
of important aspects of the trip that need
to be considered.'*

Too much controlling of structure will stifle a child just as too many open-ended scenarios provides insecurity for a child. Learn how to provide the balance and choose occasions to allow both systems to thrive.

> *'We're what we repeatedly do. Excellence then isn't an act, but a habit.'*
> **– Aristotle**

What's wrong with a little downtime in our life?

Are we fearful of hearing the words, 'I'm bored'?

As parents we work hard to provide plenty of busy activities for our children, especially after school and much of this is often sports. What we need to consider is building in downtime. Call it what you like but giving a child idle time to simply be and find their own way, without direction, is important for their emotional development.

If children choose to use this idle time in a constructive way, parents always feel better. However, sometimes it's valuable for a child just to enjoy some downtime. We all need to create balance in our life. Finding balance will only come when a child learns to understand that more relaxing times are equally important.

When teachers plan their agenda for the day, they will often include free time. This is where no demands are placed on the children and they are free to do what suits them. There is no judgement made on how they use their time. This free time creates healthy mental spaces between busy learning activities. It gives a child the chance to immerse themselves in their own thoughts and direct their own actions. Children love these times in the classroom.

When working with children who seemed quite stressed, it was common to invite them into my office and just let them be with whatever toys or activities were present. Sometimes they would just sit and enjoy the space of being in the office while I continued doing my work. It was about creating a peaceful and non-threatening moment where they focused on their thoughts.

Many of the self-disciplined practices – such as yoga, mindfulness and meditation – focus on finding yourself in your own head space. As parents, we tend to think that we need to fill those spaces with busy activities or at least advise our children as to how they could employ their spare time.

Here are some suggestions to help set the scene at home for some downtime:

- Let your child know that you enjoy downtime in your life and discuss how you find that time.
- Look at the set up at home. Are there quiet spaces that the child can find to be on their own? Consider the surrounding noises.
- Let your child situate their toys in a comfortable and accessible space. This demonstrates that you're happy for them to engage with these spontaneously as they're quite visible. Try not to lock them up all in the child's bedroom. Finding personal time can be in different parts of the house.
- I appreciate that television can be seen as downtime but watch that this is seen as one aspect of their personal time.
- If your child enjoys being outside, set the outdoor space up so that they can find themselves absorbed in outdoor activities. There isn't anything more mentally refreshing than jumping on trampolines, bouncing balls, shooting for goals, skipping, digging in small sandpits and so on. Children can really lose themselves in outdoor recreation.

- Set up routines at home to ensure that downtime is factored in. This could be that every week you decide as a family to simply have downtime. Invite your child into planning the routine of downtime.
- Talk as a family about what downtime can look like for different members of the family. What's important here is the conversation about how the family values downtime.

Downtime refreshes the spirit, clears the mental cobwebs and charges the emotional battery, ready for more active engagement with life.

> *'Time isn't the main thing. It's the only thing.'*
> **– Miles Davis**

Bedtime can be tricky

Who likes going to bed? Do I hear a resounding 'yes' from tired parents? Or maybe a reluctant 'no' because there is so much to do once your child has gone to bed? Bedtime is a tricky and difficult time for some families. If you're a family with strong, regular routines and a fair amount of house discipline, you may find this isn't an issue. However, many families –due to the different ages of children in the family and the variable nature of the week –struggle in finding that this is the best part of their day.

It was quite obvious in the school setting that some children needed more sleep than others, some went to bed with ease and anticipation and others were quite often dozing in the afternoon. You certainly don't need a lecture from me, as I also struggled with this issue as a busy parent.

When working with children, I noticed that those students who liked routine and order were, according to their parents, often able to adjust to sleeping at the same time each night. Camps proved this as some children, despite all the noise and excitement, were asleep by 8 pm!

Research tells us that regular sleep patterns and plenty of sleep are necessary for a healthy mind and body.

Consider the following ideas that may help some families in establishing reasonable bedtime routines:

- Have a family meeting and look at the plans for that week. Discuss an agreed time for bed each night; this may vary subject to family and work demands.

- Discuss what bedtime looks like for each child. Is it reading for half an hour or listening to music beforehand? It may be different for each child subject to age and interests. Daylight savings may also present different challenges for bedtime arrangements.

- Set up a chart – perhaps on the fridge – and agree to tick off each day after everyone has honoured the arrangements.

- If the night before was successful, remember to affirm everyone for their efforts. If not so successful, gently discuss what prevented the plan from working well.

Parents should also put their plans in place and use the chart to show their children how important it is to reflect on how much sleep they're getting each night.

Check your child's sleeping environment. Are there too many lights set up around the house to distract them? This also applies to noise around the house at bedtime. Sometimes children need soft lighting to assist in sleeping and you should discuss with them what makes them comfortable at bedtime. Respecting each child's feelings about sleep is important so that they understand you're listening to their concerns.

Also note that if your child is highly active before bed this could delay their ability to settle. Consider how to slow down the house stimulation before bedtime. Some parents find turning down lights is helpful to calm the home environment.

While we all desire the routine and regularity of bedtime, I believe it's best to make it a weekly family discussion so that everyone is aware that regular sleep is valued in the family.

We're all working towards maintaining the best situation possible under the pressures of the week.

Happy sleeping!

Chapter 3

Being a role model

Apologising is key

Apologising teaches your child so much about being human, never underestimate its power!

It demonstrates that you're human, not invincible and that as a parent you make mistakes. It shows your child that you're honest and that you believe in the value of honesty.

A child looks lovingly to their parents and implicitly trusts them. They're not interested in whether you're a perfect person. In fact, no one is and its best to show your child how human you are from time to time. Showing them that we're all working on improving ourselves – and this means acknowledging mistakes – is an excellent direction to give your child.

When you make a mistake that affects your child, a simple apology lets them know that at times you need to correct yourself and that this is an admirable quality. Sometimes in our anxiousness to show our best face, we can avoid the truth to look consistent and strong. Actually, your child easily senses that they're not given the truth, they can become confused and thus be given the wrong message.

By modelling this behaviour to your child, you're encouraging them to be in control at all cost and to never lose face. It's much better to show them that the human condition means that mistakes will be made and saying sorry is a way of reconciling with another person; showing your vulnerability displays your humanness.

When apologising, be explicit. Explain what behaviour led you to make that mistake. For example:

> *'I'm sorry that I forgot to attend your concert at school. I was so busy at work that I lost track of time.'*

By showing your child that you were careless, it takes the sting away from the issue and gives both of you a chance to talk it through. For example:

> *'Yes, I made a mistake, it affected you and that made you unhappy. I'm sorry.'*

Consider the following thoughts:
- A child deserves the truth.
- Being honest about mistakes breaks no trust and puts your relationship with your child in a safe and secure place.
- If a parent struggles in being honest and saying sorry, are they anxious about holding onto power? How long can they keep this going?

- You're teaching your child how to work through their problems when they make mistakes.
- Be genuine. If you say sorry ensure it's talked through with your child. By being open in this way, it reduces tension in a relationship and your child comes to expect nothing less than the truth.

The more we cover up when mistakes are made, the greater burden it is to keep up the façade. You can't fool your child. They look for honesty and expect the truth. All they want is an open and loving relationship.

In my experience, the best loved and valued teachers were those that had an authentic relationship with their children. The more the teacher showed some vulnerabilities, the more supportive and helpful the children were.

> *'Children aren't looking for perfect parents, they are looking for honest parents.'*
> **– Howard G Hendricks**

Teaching children about themselves

Growing up can be a complicated and difficult business for all of us. It's about finding out who you are and where you have come from on many different levels.

Children begin their development of self-awareness from birth and in little ways they begin to slowly develop a sense of themselves through their interactions and relationships with family and other significant people in their life.

School is a time for testing themselves against others and for building a sense of who they are in the eyes of others.

Most important is that they develop a liking of themselves and clearly mark out a space in their world. Teachers put challenges in front of children inviting them to reflect on themselves, their gifts and growth curves. This practice is a regular part of teaching.

As a parent, it's important to ensure that your child knows that you love them. Also, giving them clear understandings of where they come from and their family story is critical, as they develop a secure place in their mind of who they are and where they fit into family and society.

Here are some suggestions to give guidance to your child as they begin to develop a sense of themselves in the world:

- Always be truthful about the past. Sometimes it can be hard to hear, but a child has a right to understand where they came from and who were instrumental people in their life.
- Tell stories about the family. Perhaps there are funny situations that occurred when you were a child. Children love to store these stories in their memory, and, over time, they become special family memories.
- Talking about how you grew up and the differences in today's world is also helpful. Here you discuss the differences on a generational basis. It helps children put themselves in a context.
- When subjects come up such as Anzac Day, do you have family stories to tell? Cultural traditions are important to talk about in families.
- When giving your child an affirming message, ensure that you talk more about the quality observed in your child. For example:

'I was so impressed when you helped your brother cross the street. You have a generous streak in you.'

Here you're reminding them of their generosity which highlights a quality of your child. You're also building up images of what you see in your child. This helps them develop an image of themselves and it's all about building up their identity.

- From time to time, write little notes that emphasises the noticeable qualities that you've observed in them.
- If you have precious family heirlooms, use these objects as a chance to talk about family history. Old family photos are a great resource here.

As a parent, you have a privileged role in guiding your child into self-awareness. There will come a time when your child takes ownership of who they are, but until then, be the gentle hand leading your child into a world where they feel valued, loved and confident. So much of this comes from your mature reassurance.

Show confidence in your child

This might seem a strange topic. Especially as you might think, *I always show my child the confidence I've got in them all the time*. Our children carefully read messages that we give them both directly and indirectly. They're always looking for that special reassurance from their parents. They're keen to gain approval and the more they understand and appreciate your style of affirming them, the better.

With all of this in mind, this section is about alerting you to be consistent and clear in the way you show your child how confident you are in them.

Here are some pointers:

- Use the same words often. For example:

> *'I'm really confident in your ability to do your very best.'*

After giving such a message, ensure the follow up is equally as valid and doesn't drop in intent. For example:

> *'Great effort today. I could see how much effort you put into it.'*

- Always keep the same thread running through your conversations, especially with regard to showing confidence in their efforts. Take care that if you're making some comments about improvement, you still need to demonstrate to your child that you're confident of their ability to have ago. This confidence has in no way been compromised.

- Areas where parents can often fall down is when they comment on sport or other recreational activities. Children need encouragement and they need to feel that their best was recognised by their parent. Take care not to subtly imply that you expected more from them or that you were proud of them, but extra effort would have been better. When subtle, negative messages are conveyed in sentences like this, your child generally only hears the criticism, and the affirmation has very little value.

I know this sounds complicated, but it's actually quite simple! You say and demonstrate consistently that you have confidence in their efforts and abilities, and you understand that improvement is always part of the process. When working with children, I've seen that by demonstrating absolute, uncomplicated confidence in a child, improvement naturally occurs.

A child who feels that their parents have confidence in them, naturally take ownership of their own improvements. After all, if their parents are confident in them, everything is possible.

Being an effective listener and demonstrating justice

Many children have an over developed sense of justice when they're young. They simply can't see how others get away with not following the rules and they can get quite upset because they feel that they do the right thing and others don't. Often, they haven't yet developed strong social literacies and insightfulness. They may have a strong sense of justice about what is right and wrong, with a black and white approach.

An excellent way to help them is to resolve matters using a process called restorative practice. This is commonly used in schools. It's easily done, and it shows your children that you're listening to their concerns. Bring the family together and hear the concerns from each child, then acknowledge that you understand that they have differences. Invite them to articulate what their needs are in this situation, then invite them to agree on negotiating. This means that all children in the family compromise on an issue.

If this is an ongoing method used in families, the children soon begin to realise that this is how it works in your home. They will begin to learn that deep listening and negotiation makes it a win-win situation for everyone, and they will want to use it to ensure they have been heard. When this method is used often to resolve conflict, children learn to use the process themselves.

How can anyone argue with someone who listens and is prepared to negotiate? For a child who is heavily focused on justice, this is the best way forward.

Chapter 4

Values

The value of problem solving

Schools understand the value of teaching problem solving. The style of teaching often taught is through an inquiry-based learning approach whereby questioning and problem solving play a very big part in how children are taught to learn.

With this in mind, as a parent, teaching problem solving from an early age makes a lot of sense. Consider some of the advantages: if you're encouraging problem solving, you're inviting your child to solve their own problems and you're also encouraging independent thinking and risk taking. You are, in effect, teaching your child that making mistakes, trialling ways to solve problems and 'having a go' are valuable tools in working out how to solve life issues. As a parent, you're teaching them to rely on their own ingenuity, creativity and common sense. It also shows that you have confidence in their own decision making.

Let's look at some strategies to support your child's ability to problem solve:

- Be the role model and talk to your child about how you brainstorm issues when you have a problem. Demonstrate some recent examples of how you dealt with some problems that needed careful thought.
- Teach your child to list some options they might be thinking about to solve a problem. For example:

'Try listing three ways you could solve that problem.'

'Great, now let's discuss each option and see how it would work for you.'

- Some children enjoy having a problem-solving book where they write in optional ways to look at the problem.
- Use the what, where, why and how questions. This can be a habit to ask children when they talk about a problem. For example:

  1. **What** is the problem?
  2. **Where** is it to be dealt with?
  3. **Why** is it a problem?
  4. **How** can you solve it?

These four questions can help children think a bit deeper about the problem they aim to solve.

Another tool to help children solve problems is to simply write down the problem. Some children reflect more deeply when they see something written down on paper.

A few tips to make the process work well:

- Have faith in your child's ability to work it out. Be patient.
- Ensure that your body language is always positive when a child offers suggestions.
- Affirm their efforts. For example:

> *'Well done for thinking of that as an option.'*

- Allow them to make mistakes and reassure them that this is part of the process.
- Remind them of famous people – such as Einstein – who only learnt through practice and making errors.
- Encourage perseverance. For example:

> *'Great effort. Have you planned any further direction with that problem?'*

When working with children with regard to school issues – such as friendship problems, anxiety about poor performance and so on – it was most important to firstly talk about the success you had noticed in previous attempts. For example:

> *'I know we're talking about how you want friends. I'm thinking of how you played happily with John and Michael last term. That seemed like a great friendship.'*

This is all about giving your child an awareness that they have had success before.

Problem solving isn't always a neat process and does require revisiting issues and understanding that risk taking can lead to some failure. However, once a child values owning their problems and enjoys the process of trial and error with brainstorming and open and supportive discussion, their emotional growth takes an amazing leap. Let's not forget how intellectually stimulating it is as a process of learning.

> *'A problem well put is half solved'*
> **– John Dewey**

The value of helping others

How quickly we can take helping others for granted and forget the absolute value there is in learning to help others. This is an important area to teach our children and we should never presume it will automatically happen.

School focuses on the importance of children working together, cooperating through group work and it strategically teaches children the value of supporting each other.

However, this isn't enough. A child needs to learn by example from home that helping others is seen as a critical dimension of family life.

This kind of helping is about developing selflessness and touches on learning about empathy for the other person. As a family, there are many occasions where a child will see examples of family members helping each other. It's also a time for children to learn about helping others outside their comfort zones.

Here are some strategies that may be helpful in strengthening the notion of helping others:

- Discuss as a family on a regular basis how help was given when needed. For example:

  > *'Thanks for helping me clean the garage. It was a lot of work for just one person.'*

- When you hear of examples of your child helping others, affirm the act and acknowledge the difference it made for that person.
- Read about kind acts and good deeds that you may find in the newspaper, in books or movies seen together. Children need to understand that helping others can happen in many and varied forms.
- Set up a helping book. This is where a child records occasions where they were able to support others. This is great for a discussion.
- Helping others may mean being less selfish, which is a wonderful growth curve for a child. When you notice how a child has been helpful and you observe that there was some self-sacrifice in it, affirm that fact. For example:

  > *'When you helped your mum with the dishes, you had less time for your special television show. How considerate are you!'*

- Play family games where you need to rely on each other. This teaches your child that working as a team is best for everyone.

- Pose questions that require your child to solve based on helping others. For example:

   'Can you think of ways we can help your little brother learn to walk? What can we do to help him?'

- Be spontaneous in affirming your child when you see them helping others. For example:

   'I noticed that you gave up sitting in the front seat of the car as you wanted to settle down your brother who was upset. That was a such a kind thing to do.'

- Read books to your child about people who were known for their kindness. There are many suitable children's books about such people.
- Talk about family members who show kindness and are known for their helpfulness. Discuss why they are such liked members of the family.

Never underestimate the value in teaching a child the importance of being helpful.

The value of being proactive

How many times in our daily interactions with our children do we become reactive or emotionally charged when disasters have happened? This is quite normal in our busy, complicated lives and when the incident happens, behaviour deteriorates. We naturally react; after all, it has to be dealt with and sometimes on the spot! Unfortunate words are said, regrets then follow and we become concerned that we have damaged our relationship with our children. Does this sound like a normal scenario in your house? Parents would often tell me how tired they felt after these confrontations.

Here I'll discuss the art of being proactive. I refer to it as an 'art', as it takes practice and skill to avoid problems, foresee tricky situations and carefully negotiate your way around them.

Being proactive has some wonderful outcomes both for child and parent:

- It slows down everyone's anxiety.
- It makes for a calmer environment – a quieter and less disruptive house.
- It reduces conflict. Everyone enjoys freedom from conflict.
- It provides opportunities to affirm your child rather than disciplining them following an incident.
- It makes for less reaction and children feel more secure and less conscious of making mistakes.

There is so much going for being proactive.

Here are some suggestions on learning the art of being proactive:

- Check your daily plan. Are there occasions where your child could be unsettled? For example, supermarket visits. Is it possible to change schedules where they could be excluded from them?
- Be aware of fatigue levels. If the activities planned are physically demanding and back-to-back, perhaps

reduce activities so they cope better. Fatigue can be an immediate trigger for the change in a child's behaviour.

- Attending meetings or appointments in the morning is always less stressful for children. Be organised and plan. Take happy distractions with you when attending appointments or meetings.
- Talk to your child before going out in the day. Let them know what will happen and let them suggest how they can plan to be content and fulfilled during events.
- If you have some news to tell them that will cause some anxiety, think through how you will talk to them and choose the appropriate time and place to chat.
- At the end of the day check in with them. For example:

> *'Thanks for being helpful today. I was able to get all the things done we needed to do.'*

- Look at the layout of your house. Is it set up to ensure less accidents? It's amazing how rearranging furniture can impact on a child's ability to cope in the house. Teachers would often rearrange desks and tables to introduce a new way of just being in the classroom.
- If sibling fighting is occurring more than normal, check where the children are situated. Are they visible to you? Are there occasions where they can be separated to reduce tension? Do you know the triggers to the dispute?

- Is your yard set up for activities that the children can enjoy and be active? Home yards are great environments in which to de-stress when tension mounts in the house. Even short five-minute breaks reduce the pressure between children.

- Short, sharp breaks with your children help ward off incidents. For example, if you're in the shopping centre, can you stop and have a break to stop the mounting tension?

- Sometimes it's a matter of stopping the activity midstream so that you don't become reactive when behaviour is deteriorating. Read the signs that your child gives you.

- Check on your own capabilities, wellness and fatigue. If you're not able to positively manage the day's activities can things be changed or simply reduced?

- Use simple 'I' statements to alert your child about the situation. For example:

'I'm feeling unwell at the moment.
Please play outside and I'll talk to you later
about the matter.'

When working with children, it was most important to engage with them when I felt ready, had adequate time and was able to offer something positive in the conversation. While this sounds ideal, the point here was to not destroy the relationship by being reactive in how I spoke due to being rushed or distracted.

Teachers are well aware that to get the best from their children, their personal readiness, wellness and mental fitness is necessary, otherwise chaos can prevail and then they deal with reactive behaviours for the whole day.

> *'Being successful requires being proactive and not waiting for life to come to you. It means you're on offense. Not defence. You're active not passive.'*
> – Benjamin P Hardy

It's all about how we value children

I have said that you could write a PHD on the following: in my office my 'feelings chart' is used quite often. The one feeling children always talk about is the feeling of 'being proud'.

When this response is examined, the deeper meaning concerns the child's feelings that their actions aren't making their parents proud. This might seem strange, as we might think that we reinforce them often. But this is sometimes why children are reluctant to 'have a go'. Will they fail? What will people think?

A good response to these questions is to often remind them of the things that make you proud. For example:

'I'm so proud of your efforts at school'.

'I'm proud that you had a go at something hard.'

Even though we acknowledge their efforts, they're always checking in with us as to whether they're valued. Using the word 'proud' has high value in their minds.

Chapter 5

How to influence your child's behaviour

Motivating children to change behaviour

Who wants to change their behaviour when you can't find any reason to change? Think about your own situation. No amount of pressure motivates you to change your behaviour unless you see the value in the way it affects you or makes a difference. We're all motivated by change when it has relevance and serves a purpose that we understand.

How many times do you find yourself repeating the same instructions to your child and your level of frustration continues to grow, sometimes disproportionately to the situation? Repeated requests or instructions to do something becomes less effective as time goes on. A child's listening drops off and all sorts of distractions coincidentally get in the way for the child. No surprises there!

Here are some thoughts on how best to change behaviour that you believe is important to change:

- Always check in with yourself and establish if changing the behaviour is necessary. There are degrees of necessity. For example, do you want your child's room cleaned straight away and the dishes complete or something more substantial like cooperating to get to school on time?

- Remember that your child needs to value the change or at least see that the changed behaviour had an impact on you. For example:

> *'Can you leave the mat outside the front door? This way I can wipe my feet and not slip in the kitchen.'*

Notice here that you're letting them know that their support will have a positive impact on you. Your child may, after all, have little motivation to adjust the mat. However, they are more inclined to cooperate if it makes a difference to you.

- Be clear in what you ask. Repeated instructions with increased agitation only cause shutdowns and major meltdowns on your part. If your child doesn't listen and change the behaviour, you will need to sit them down and approach the request from a different angle. Simply telling them how disappointed you are won't motive change in their behaviour.
- Take care not to expect a consistent change in behaviour as this can become more robotic. Children are, after all, human and when they do respond to your request, take care to thank them. For example:

> *'Thanks for helping with your little brother. I now have more time to myself.'*

- Consider how much change in behaviour you're seeking in any one day, morning or afternoon block. Too much preoccupation in giving instructions loses its momentum after a while.

- Choose your language carefully and reflect on what you're asking them to do. Is the expectation too high? Are they in a frame of mind to manage the changed behaviour or are they preoccupied? Timing is everything and you want success rather than a feeling of your child not listening and responding.

- Keep in mind fatigue and their ability to listen on a particular occasion. Sometimes their readiness to change isn't present. Therefore, how important is it to press the issue of change?

- Affirm and acknowledge their efforts in supporting change regularly. For example:

*'Thanks for tidying the kitchen yesterday.
Cooking is now so much easier.'*

When working with children, timing was a key factor in attempting to change behaviour. Teachers are always conscious to notice children spontaneously changing behaviour in the classroom and affirming it. It's given a great deal of attention in the class when a child shows real growth in changing what is seen as inappropriate behaviour.

Similarly, if your child recognises that they need to improve or change behaviour and they do it independently, that's cause for celebration; a time to acknowledge how they thought about the impact they had on others. This is simply learning about empathy.

Here is an example:

> *'I always enjoy listening to my music,
> but it will wake the baby.'*

Here we tell the child that 'I need to change my behaviour as it will have an impact on another.'

> *'Fortunately, most human behaviour is learnt
> observationally through modelling from others.'*
> **– Albert Bandura**

Learn to be a coach, not an instructor

Coaches are there to guide and give advice gained from their well-earned experience and training over many years. They're valued because they're not forcing their opinions on you; they're merely giving you the wisdom of their knowledge. They're quite unemotional when it comes to giving advice, but they weigh up all the options in the light of all the information given to them and invite their client to consider the various proposals they make.

A coach is significantly beneficial because they are an advisory body and they leave it to the client to decide if, how and when they will proceed with suggestions.

Consider taking on the role of coach with your child. This will involve being less in control of decisions made for your child and more reflective on looking at options. A child will always value a parent who uses less power and includes them when making decisions. Being a consultant takes practice on the part of the parent and can be a trial-and-error process. A parent can start with a child from an early age. For example:

> *'I've been looking at all your toys. Some are dangerous when you walk on them and some are soft. These are the dangerous ones. If you packed the dangerous ones away first it would mean you won't hurt yourself.'*

Here you're stating what you know about the safety of the toys. You point out which one is dangerous when walking around and you then leave the decision to your child to move that toy first.

When working with children at school, it was common practice to put the options on the table, discuss the pros and cons and then leave the decision to the child. This gives them more ownership of their decisions and they begin to recognise that using the information gained is beneficial to their outcomes. Once a child develops a taste for being a significant part of making their decisions, they usually act very reliably to ensure they take further ownership of decisions. Here is another example:

> *'I hear you want to walk home from school on your own. Let's look at some factors that concern me and then we can discuss what's possible.'*

Note here, as a consultant, you're putting forward experienced reasons why this decision may not suit. Using this approach, your child is more likely to value your opinions and be more tolerant of the negative reasons you present.

If you only talk about all the negative reasons why they can't walk home, they're not included in the decision, which to them may seem unjust and also too much use of power on your behalf. By putting forward your cases and debating all the reasons – both positive and negative – your child will feel included in the final decision.

Sometimes being a coach can involve putting forward your knowledge about a matter that is under discussion. For example, if your child talks about smoking, it's a chance to simply state your views on smoking backed by some facts. Such coaching can happen incidentally. It doesn't challenge anything particularly; it merely outlines your knowledge and beliefs about a matter under discussion. Teachers throughout the week will often talk about facts and leave the thinking up to the children.

When working with children, after deciding what they would want to work on, they would then set goals. A helpful mechanism was to suggest that they set a goal with a timeline and a plan to check in afterwards.

Teachers will work with children to set goals for the term. Such goals are discussed later in the term with the child and parent. There are no expectations placed on the child, rather they set the plan with parental guidance with no pressure attached.

Coaching is about assisting a child to make decisions guided comfortably by your knowledge and experience. It's not intrusive. It allows them to think for themselves but with responsible guidance.

Don't linger on your child's behaviour

From time to time, we all feel disappointed in our children's behaviour. If we're a structured and self-disciplined person sometimes it's hard to understand how our children can operate quite differently to us. Accepting behaviour that is different to ours, perhaps even embarrassing and hard to understand, can sometimes bring us down.

Where did that child come from? After all, I didn't give them that bad example of poor behaviour. It certainly doesn't come from me.

We need to put things into perspective here. When a child misbehaves, they're being children and acting as a child would act when unsettled about something. The behaviour you witness – like everyone's behaviour – is driven by an issue that unsettles them and what you see is the manifestation of their upset feelings. It's only behaviour and should not be internalised as something with a deeper, more sinister meaning.

Sometimes we only see the poor behaviour and we attempt to overanalyse it, concentrating on the unattractive aspects of the behaviour.

'Perhaps my child has a deeper problem?'

'Are we setting a poor example?'

'I need to be stricter.'

'What must people think of us?'

'Is he getting that behaviour from school?'

I'm not discussing the nature of the problem which leads to the behaviour, rather it's about our response to the behaviour and how we come to understand it for what it really is: childlike behaviour.

Here are some thoughts on how to respond:

- Be calm and steady when an incident happens, it's only an incident. It will pass. Tomorrow is another day.
- Remember that once the problem is solved, you need to move on and not continue to reflect on the poor behaviour. For the child, it's passed once resolved.
- A child will be quite unsettled if you continue to harbour on the poor behaviour. For them it was their meltdown and what is more important is the resolution of the problem, not the nature of the meltdown.
- Take care not to talk around your child about how disappointed you were and how you don't want to see that behaviour again.
- A child may have different problems and manifest them in different behavioural ways. Don't expect that this pattern will change. When a new problem comes along, they could have a completely different response to it subject to age, tiredness and circumstance.

Teachers are very skilled in moving on from children's poor behaviour. While they don't like the experience, they recognise that it will pass once dealt with and in order to keep the relationship with their student, they need to demonstrate that they've moved on. They will quickly give positive reinforcement to emphasise to children that they're valued despite the poor behaviour.

I'm not suggesting that poor behaviour is tolerated, rather, that it needs to be understood. A parent should be a good listener and should problem solve to resolve the matter. Don't let feelings of resentment linger in your mind.

Parent's expectations and a child's place in the family

What a big and messy topic this can become!

Most parents will tell a teacher that they expect high but realistic expectations for their child's achievements. Most parents will also tell you that they regularly affirm their children's work and that they encourage them to do their best. They will also add that at no point do they criticise their children for poor work. However, some children still feel undervalued and unsuccessful which can lead to lack of motivation.

This is a tricky problem if you're a parent just wanting the best for your child!

When I worked with children struggling with their perceived lack of performance and personal image, the following was clearly evident:

- The child had felt that their parents weren't proud of them. They also believed that what they did wasn't making them valued the way that they wanted to be valued.

- Their perception was a blocker for parents who thought that they were affirming their children adequately.

The answer can be quite complex, but the following tools can help parents in presenting a strong image of support for their child. These tools have worked well with some families.

Try using the following:

- Always talk about the positive using an 'I' statement. For example:

> *'I appreciate all your efforts today.'*

> *'I like the work you've done.
> I can see all the effort you've made.'*

Also occasionally saying:

> *'Sometimes I found it hard to do well myself and I feel so glad that you're having a go at everything you do. This makes me proud.'*

The emphasis here is on the child understanding that their work has had an impact on you. For some children, this extra parental reinforcement is necessary.

Affirming simple activities that we take for granted can also be helpful in reassuring children. For example:

> *'Thanks for helping me with the groceries.
> I'm not as tired now.'*

> *'I love your smile. It makes me happy.'*

Some children just need more affirmation and reassurance that they're valued. It may not be the case for all the children in your family; some need less personal reassurance.

Every child has their own emotional journey. Sometimes the order of the family can have an impact on where you see yourself, being an only child or just dealing with strong sibling personalities, can shape your perceptions. Whatever the reason, every child will respond to their parents differently, subject to how emotionally secure they feel in the eyes of their parents.

Keep in mind:

- How you treat each child in the family may require different tactics.
- No child is a mirror image of their siblings.
- Every child listens carefully for parental reassurance, some listen more closely and need to hear it more often.

In any one classroom, there would be many children all seeking attention on different levels. Some were more needy, more vocal and others more at peace in just listening and responding in a calmer way. Teachers expect that how they respond to each child will require different approaches; so too are a family's expectations for responding to different children's needs.

How do we build resilience in our children?

A big question that many parents ask themselves is, 'How do we make our children more resilient?' While there are many support programs at school that we can use to help our children, one powerful strategy is to let your child see how resilient we are as parents in our own life.

How we influence our children is best done by modelling our own strength in coping with difficult situations. Positive language we use in discussing a problem gives your child the awareness that you're calmly reflecting and can approach a situation from many angles. It's about a 'no blame' outlook.

For example, when faced with some crisis try using phrases like:

'I have a problem and I need time to think it through.'

'I need to look at different ways to sort this out.'

'At the moment I'm working through some troubling issues.'

This is about giving your child the message that there can be many ways to solve a problem and that having a problem is normal. Staying calm during that time and looking at many angles of the situation is the best way forward.

When I've dealt with children in areas around resilience, it's not uncommon to hear them talk about how their parents would handle the situation. If they have parents who look at quick solutions and blame, it's harder for their child to take personal ownership of their situation. When they recognise that their parents will look at how to resolve a situation through reflection and negotiation, the child is more receptive to owning and dealing with the problem themselves.

Children should see failure as a part of success

This certainly sounds contradictory! However, what's important to remember here is that failure happens all the time. Failures happens when a child tries to open a jar with a firm lid, knocks over blocks or is failing at school with friendships or learning in the classroom; it can seem like a daily event.

But let's teach our children that failure is an acceptable way of growing and learning. It's a natural part of our life occurring on a regular basis. Einstein would say that unless he failed in his experiments regularly, he wouldn't learn where to go next in his work.

As a parent, we work hard to affirm and reassure our children that they can succeed. However, we should teach them that through our mistakes, we can grow and succeed. Failure is a sign that we have discovered an area in which to grow.

One of the best ways to do this is to use your own examples:

'Gosh, I've tried to make that recipe work but, sadly, I failed. I'll get some advice from my friend who seems to make it so well.'

'Sadly, I wasn't successful in that job application. I'll ask them what skills I needed so that I can improve my application next time.'

'I missed that turn off on the freeway. I'll have to pay more attention to the road signs in future'.

The previous examples illustrate that while you weren't successful, you would use the experience to gain more insight. This is the key: teaching children that through error we find new ways to learn.

Don't forget to applaud a child when they attempt to work through their failure. For example:

> 'Well done. When you saw that you didn't do well on that spelling test you checked in with the teacher for help. Bravo!'

In the school setting, teachers would often affirm children when they demonstrated that they had developed ways to work through their own problems. This was about taking ownership for their failures and understanding how to get the best from that experience.

When working with children who were anxious about failure, it was quite common to chat about the times they had succeeded by working through a problem. It was about training them to recognise the value in just 'having another go', finding a new way forward or experimenting with options. For example:

> 'You didn't find a friend in the yard when the bell went, but you went looking for someone new anyway. That was a clever way of moving on.'

Children need to recognise failure as a growth curve where they will embark on a new strategy to work through the problem. This makes them successful. Of course, everything within reason.

> *'Anyone who has never made a mistake has never tried anything new.'*
> **– Albert Einstein**

Setting goals

Is setting goals something that you do during your week?

Indirectly or directly, we're always planning ahead, and we understand that in order to achieve certain outcomes by the end of the week, we need to complete some goals. For example, if we want to have a special dinner party on the weekend, we know that we need to plan the menu, go shopping for ingredients and so on. Sometimes, we're unaware that we actually set goals for ourselves because we become very efficient at processing how to meet our needs. This section is about helping a child to value the planning process and to recognise how setting goals gives us control of ourselves and our lives through self-discipline.

At the beginning of the week, ask your child what they would like to achieve – perhaps at school – by the end of the week. Once they give some indication of what they would like to achieve, talk about setting a pathway to get to that point. For example, your child may be really keen to play soccer after school on Thursday; that's their goal and tell them it's a goal. Ask them, 'What do you need to do before you can achieve that goal?' Perhaps it's completing homework or chores. Here we're simply encouraging the child to set realistic goals. When they achieve their goals, they gain the satisfaction of celebrating their contributions and they own the process of achieving their goal.

Teachers are well aware that when a child sets goals in their work, they discuss with them the steps to be taken to reach that goal. For example, if a child wants their spelling to improve, they may set up a plan to learn words each night, get parents to help them and so on. They design and own the strategies to achieve their goal and that gives them all the satisfaction. They also learn to evaluate their steps and next time become more astute in choosing the best path to achieve their goals.

As a parent, encourage your child to set simple goals. This could be with regard to home or school. Encourage them to plan out how they will achieve their goal. Make it simple to begin with and your child will learn the value of setting goals and be conditioned to doing it more regularly.

When working with children who were showing some anxiety about schoolwork, I would first ask them to be clear about what aspects of their work were causing them issues. I would then ask them to talk about strategies they had used in the past or would like to use to set the goal of feeling better about their work. Once they thought about it, I was amazed how they took more control of their problem. They started to control their anxiety.

As a parent, you can help by listening and discussing their strategies to achieve their goal. Talking to them about your own personal goals and how you set them up will help them reflect on the positive impact goal setting has had in your life.

Encourage them along the way. Listen, affirm and applaud them when they have a go at achieving a goal. Remember, the point of this exercise is training children to value setting goals as a means to achieve their ends. The motivation behind setting the goal and finding strategies to achieve that goal is a key driver throughout this process.

Confronting poor behaviour

This is something that parents face regularly. One of the questions parents ask is, 'How do I deal with an issue and at the same time avoid damaging the relationship with my child?' Firstly, let me assure you that your child innately knows that you love them unconditionally. Sometimes how we act can confuse them and even if you lose your temper and react negatively, they do believe in your absolute love for them.

Having said that, less damage is caused by creating a situation where you let your child know how disappointed you are in the behaviour because it has impacted on some aspect of your family life.

Consider the following tips to help deal with confrontation and still keep the relationship between you and your child a happy one:

- Choose a calm time to talk about the incident that's upsetting you. Reacting straightaway can cause you to overreact and anger interferes with rational conversation. If the timing isn't right, say:

'I'm upset right now, so we'll talk about this a little later.'

This gives you space to be more rational, calm and less hostile when talking to your child. Sometimes, you have time to gather more understandings around the situation which can reduce the problem and your anger. Be consistent and follow through with a conversation. Have the discussion with your child with no one else around, in a quiet space and where your child is more inclined to listen. This is all about setting the best scene to get the best results from the conversation.

- Choose a time in the morning to talk to your child because their attention span and calmness is at its peak. For example:

> *'I'd like to talk to you about something that happened recently that's upset me.'*

Once the issue is understood and resolved in some way, it's most important to acknowledge the process that you just went through and affirm your child for being part of it. For example:

> *'Thanks for working through the problem that was upsetting me. Together we were able to sort it all out.'*

Keep in mind that once the resolution is made, it's important to move on, affirm your child and give them the benefit of the doubt that they can solve problems.

When working with children over issues, I found it most important that the child knew the issue was dealt with and the relationship was back to normal. This is all about the child feeling valued – despite mistakes made.

What do we do when we don't like the behaviour?

Have you ever felt negatively about your child? Some parents tell me that they often feel guilty when they have negative feelings about their child, but this is quite natural. What you're feeling is just a dislike for their behaviour which can be unsettling, embarrassing and tiring. What we need to remember is that it's just the behaviour and not the child that unsettles us.

When working with children, I often notice that the particular look a child has on their face can influence whether people either believe or doubt them. Sometimes these expressions can be misleading as they represent feeling insecure and uncertain, and they're not reflective of indifference. I recommend not judging a child's expression, as it often just reflects an inability to deal with the situation.

As a parent, think about the following when feeling unsettled about a behaviour:

- *I love my child, but I don't like the behaviour.* Therefore, just talk about the behaviour. For example:

> *'I really don't like what just happened.*
> *We need to understand what really happened so*
> *that we can move on.'*

- Always reaffirm the child after working through the behaviour. This reassures them that everything is back to normal.
- Sometimes writing notes of reassurance gives your child a feeling that you've moved on. The note could say,

> *'Thanks for solving that problem that was on my mind. Now we can look forward to …'*

It's all about separating the behaviour from the child, reassuring them that we move on from mistakes and grow through the process, therefore maintaining a healthy, long-lasting relationship.

Chapter 6

Parenting

Who agrees with who in parenting?

Have you discovered since becoming a parent how different you can be to your partner when it comes to parenting styles? This is quite common in families.

When I facilitated parent courses, it was quite common to hear parents say that their styles of parenting were quite different. Often, it was based on how they were brought up. This can be quite daunting for couples who think they are compatible on so many levels! Often, we don't think about how we will react as a parent to our child's behaviour until it actually happens.

It's quite normal to have different approaches to rearing a child. After all, it's hard to change how you understand child rearing, given your own journey as a child, be it positive or negative. The key approach is to agree that at times you will have different understandings of the problem at hand. Your child knows this and, no surprises, they gravitate around the parent that is less punitive and has better listening skills. After all, didn't we do that ourselves when growing up?

Consider the following when managing different parenting styles:

- Both parents should talk to their child recognising that sometimes either parent may see matters differently and that this is normal.
- Agree that sometimes some issues will be allocated to one parent and vice versa. Of course, all issues will be discussed as a family.
- What is most important is that the child doesn't side with one parent over the other. This is where it gets complicated. Children are very aware of how parents can have different opinions on matters pertaining to all sorts of things such as homework, staying out late, tidiness and so on.

Whoever deals with the issue should maintain the following:

- Listen effectively.
- Respond calmly and then actively listen to the concern.
- After agreeing to understand the issue, start negotiating. In the negotiation stage, this is where parents may have different expectations, and this is okay.
- If both parents use this same approach, the child will feel that they have been spoken to fairly and consistently. They will also recognise that while parents have different expectations, they still listen and negotiate in the same way.

This topic was the cause of much discussion in my parent groups and we all agreed that sometimes it was better to let one parent deal with certain situations as they were less emotive or at least more familiar with the matter under discussion.

In summary, parents should use the same method of working though the problem and negotiate with your interests or investments to be included.

Improvement and achievement – where do they begin and end?

Have you noticed how praise is important on so many levels? We all need praise, no matter what age! This section is about understanding that we need to be specific when we give praise. We need to ensure that we know the purpose for praise and that we target it well. For example:

'Well done on your test.
All that preparation made a great difference. Bravo!'

In order to improve and to achieve, we need to feel reassured that our efforts are truly valued. We need reassurance. The more we target our praises, the closer we get to giving the child an authentic acknowledgement, one which will make a real difference. For example:

'What a wonderful effort you made to clean the
kitchen. Every item has been put away in the
right spot. Thank you'

By being specific, your child will be aware that you're grateful for a particular task. It shows that you've clearly thought it through and that it has real value to you. By being authentic in your praise, they understand that their achievement was sincerely based on your awareness of their deeds.

General praise such as:

> *'You're a good boy,'*

has little value compared to:

> *'What a good boy you are for opening the door while I've got groceries in my hands.'*

Improvement is best understood and more likely to continue when the child clearly understands the value of their deeds. Teachers are aware of this and they're conscious to speak clearly and acknowledge children's work as specifically as possible.

When working with children, I observed that affirming with real definition builds their sense of self-confidence. For example:

> *'Thanks, Mark, for shutting the door quietly. It often jams.'*

Here the child recognises that they supported your real concerns about the door, it's incidental but an effective affirmation. This sets the scene for a confident and healthy discussion to follow. Reassurance builds on reassurance and success.

Keep in mind that through your example in praising and affirming, your child is more inclined to model this in how they affirm others. It's all about giving the best example through our communication style.

What makes an effective parent?

Parenting well can be a tricky game. We all want to do the best in our parenting and yet we must recognise that we're human and sometimes factors come into play that limit our capabilities.

The good news is that, if handled well, it's not that complicated. Here are some pointers:

- The first and foremost factor in effective parenting is to be authentic with your child. This means being honest and realistic as to who you are and what you can capably achieve. The child actually works this out at an early age themselves! For example, you can't attend a parent meeting because of work:

    'I'm disappointed that I'll miss that meeting. I'll follow up with the teacher to see what I missed.'

    Being authentic tells your child that what they see and hear from you is what they get.

- Maintain a warm and affectionate relationship with your child. This means listening to them and not being judgemental when you hear about incidents that can be unsettling.

- By listening well, you're showing sensitivity and respect to the needs and feelings of your child. This means that they will engage with you more openly in the future.

- Be a negotiator. When your child talks about issues they want addressed, discuss options openly. Some may not be acceptable to you but somewhere through discussion, a way forward can be found. For example:

  'I'm not feeling happy about you coming home that late. I can pick you up at ... and that way you can still see your friend.'

- Sometimes, confronting negative behaviour is necessary. Talk about it through an 'I' statement.

  'I'm disappointed that you ...'

- When dealing with the consequences, try and engage your child in finding a way forward. For example:

  'Do you have any suggestions to move forward?'

- Remember it's all about restoring relationships when dealing with negative behaviour. It's about both the parent and child understanding the behaviour and agreeing to an appropriate solution.
- Set boundaries for your child that are manageable for the whole family. Discuss with your child the agreed boundaries and, as time goes, discuss how they're working out as a family. Children need boundaries but will understand them better if they're given reasons for the boundaries.

For example:

> *'I need you home after school by 4.00 pm because I believe this is a reasonable and safe time to be home.'*

> *'We can't have any toys in the living room because people will trip and hurt themselves.'*

- Finally, your child loves you unconditionally. For them to embrace you in your work as a parent, be natural and let them see how genuine you are when you make mistakes by acknowledging when you're wrong. Above all, let them see how you value a strong relationship with them.

I invite you as a parent to reflect on who you gravitated around as a child in your family. I feel certain that it was the parent who listened to you unconditionally.

Don't be a probing parent

We're all trying our best to be the parent who knows everything about their children.

After all, the more we know, the more we can help.

Well, maybe. There's a fine line to this. Sometimes our children can shut down on us when asking questions as:

> *'How was school today?'*

And you only get this response:

> *'Good.'*

Parents often think that when they receive this answer their children are either disengaged or hopeful that you will just go away!

As an adult, are you always keen to answer questions at work and at home? Sometimes we just want questions to go away and this is also the case with our children. Sometimes they're just not ready to answer the question.

We need to be careful about how we ask questions. If they're constant, repetitive and irritating, a child will shut down. Probing questions are evident when we keep at an issue and ask about it in several ways. For example:

'Where did you go?'

'What did you do then?'

'What did they say?'

So, what's the best way to engage with your child?

The best way to keep your child engaged is firstly to respect the fact that sometimes they're just not ready to answer questions. This can be for many reasons, including feeling inadequate or anxious about the consequences, tired or simply wanting some space from the issue. This latter point is often the case just after school.

It's best to pose questions in an open-ended way with no set expectation of an answer. For example:

'I was wondering how you went today?'

> *'When you're ready, let me know how you
> went on that test.'*

> *'Sounds like your day was very busy.
> I wonder what made it so busy?'*

Note here that there is an invitation to respond instead of a probing question or demand. It implies, *I'm really interested in the issue, but I'm happy to hear about it when you're ready to respond.*

When working with children, it was important to phrase questions or inquiries in similar, non-probing or threatening terms. For example:

> *'Today it sounds like you had some troubles.
> I wonder what went right and what went wrong?'*

The more you invite responses with no direct or demanding expectation for an answer and instead as if you're pondering and wondering, the more likely you'll receive a response.

Here are some tips:

- Take care to only ask one question at a time. Several questions asked at once can be overwhelming.
- Be relaxed when posing the questions where no intimidation is apparent in your body language.
- If you're feeling anxious or tired, consider the suitability of the timing in asking the questions and consider how important the question is at the time for your child. You'll be more successful in

getting responses when they don't have too many preoccupations.

- It's also helpful to thank your child for giving you an answer. For example:

> *'Thanks for keeping me informed.*
> *I now know why you were late.'*

- Remember that a child responds best to warmth and non-threatening situations where they feel there is no judgement. Posing probing questions can put blame onto your child and make them feel anxious.
- Keep yourself consistently positive as best as possible to preserve the relationship.

Nine parenting tips to make life easier

Consider just how busy you are on many different levels. You want to get the very best from your relationship with your child but sometimes struggle to enjoy the experience due to family pressures, work or exhaustion. As parents, the time flies quickly and before you know it, your three-year-old has turned five and then eight and so it goes. Parents often feel regret about missed opportunities due to demands on them and limited time. All these feelings that you have as a busy parent are quite normal – and I would add healthy – as you reflect on them growing up.

Over the years I've observed many families' habits in designing family structures to find time with children. I've also experienced my own journey in finding ways to spend more time with my children.

Here are some thoughts on how to remain sane and enjoy your child even though the clock ticks so fast:

1. Slow down. This may seem impossible but try and find some aspects of the week where you can reduce or slow down some activities. If you look at the week ahead, you might find activities that could be pushed to the next week or simply taken out. The more you reduce the business, the more space you will find for your child.
2. Start uncluttering. Ensuring a simpler environment and an uncomplicated house can reduce your workload. You may notice your child more often. The Swedish are very good at keeping things simple: just consider Ikea! This is something I will discuss in further detail in Chapter 13.
3. Set up a chart with a 'tune in' date included each week where you simply spend time with your child. If you have several children, perhaps this can be done over several weeks.
4. Always check in with yourself to establish how you've engaged with your child on a particular week. Have you had a meaningful conversation? Have you laughed and cuddled together? This can be a helpful way for us to catch up if we have neglected some personal time with our child.
5. Reading to your child at night is wonderful for spending quality time together. With a larger family, try reading to all of your children once or twice a week. Choose a novel that you can enjoy together.

6. If you have family routines like walking the dog, gardening and so on, try to include your child in that activity. This is a wonderful time to share together. Even hanging washing on the line is a great shared time to talk.
7. If you've had a busy week and haven't made much personal time to talk, write a note to your child and leave it under their pillow, in their lunch box or anywhere that will surprise them. Little surprises like this can enliven your experiences together.
8. Ask your child to make suggestions of times you can connect together. You will be surprised at the array of ideas that they will present.
9. Find a special interest that just you and your child share together. I know of one family who has a special jigsaw puzzle set up on a table that only dad and the child work on together.

This is about reducing regret for missed opportunities, capitalising on occasions and modifying your routines in order to find precious time with your child.

> *'If you want your child to turn out well, spend twice as much time with them. And half as much money.'*
> **– Abigail Van Buren**

Children learning about special national events

How do you explain National Days to your children?

Across the year, we celebrate several important events in our country's calendars. Some have considerable sentiment that is felt by many across the nation such as Anzac Day or Remembrance Day.

Children read their parent's emotional state and their sincerity very well, particularly around events that touch the soul. Let us call this 'generational lessons', where we bring them into acknowledging events such as Remembrance Day.

What we pass on is an awareness of how important it is to remember, even though we may not have been personally touched by the event that led to the celebration. This is about building national pride in what is a nation's tapestry of celebrations depicting important events that are imprinted in our ever-evolving culture.

Do we have a responsibility to pass on the message of these celebrations? I would argue yes, as we owe it to our children to understand the journey of our country and to invite them to take ownership of it when they're adults.

Schools are conscious to celebrate these important events and often common signs and symbols are used to depict the day. For example, we wear a red poppy on November 11th to signify remembering the impact of World War I.

Here are some tips on how to gradually raise awareness of these national events that occur across the year:

- Have a family diary and write in these days to celebrate across the year together.
- When the day approaches, find relevant and age-appropriate books to read to your children. As they grow older, articles in the newspaper and online cover the subject well.

- Take your children to any public events that might be celebrating the day. For example, a trip to a war memorial around Anzac Day
- As a family, you can watch marches and parades on television that tell a tale about the day.
- Talk about particular symbols and what they mean. For example, what is the one-minute of silence all about?
- Why do we see Anzac biscuits on sale around Anzac Day?
- Invite your child to write down their feelings about the day and what it means to them.
- Children love symbols. Purchase items such as poppies to wear on the day. They easily can identify with symbols that tell a story.
- Check in with what the school is doing to celebrate the event. Often homework is set about understanding the significance of the day.
- Sometimes younger children become confused when they hear the word 'celebration'. After all, isn't it a sad day that we reflect on? This will need some explanation as a parent. We remind them that we celebrate the memory of the day which we hope to keep alive each year in our heart and mind.

As we say on Anzac Day:

'Lest we forget.'

As a parent, you're passing on the legacy of not forgetting.

Chapter 7

Enjoying the moment

Capture the moment and savour the experience

If you read anything about mindfulness, you will learn that it's about finding peace and harmony in the moment. As parents, we're fanatically busy rearing our children, providing for their lifestyle and planning for the future: *everything will be better if we just ... or when we just ...*

Do we ever get the chance to stop and savour an actual moment with our child? They're growing mentally, physically, emotionally and intellectually at a very fast pace. Just look at the photos you take from month to month. Reflect on your older children and ask yourself, *where have the years gone?*

This is simply an encouragement to stop and smell the roses.

When your child is being themselves, just stop and enjoy. Perhaps linger longer as you reflect on their childish ways. We don't need to wait for the cute moments and capture them on camera; just enjoy the beauty of your child in the moment. Be mindful of their presence as they settle into you for a cuddle or settle into bed with a book. How about just observing them play?

Think about the beauty that you have in your life through their existence and savour that moment. The days, weeks and years go quickly so seize the moment. You will feel better for the experience and start building a beautiful image of your child.

Sometimes, through adversity comes a simple appreciation of things. When a child is very ill and then recovers, we really begin to appreciate their presence and joy.

Try not to get trapped in negative memories or to stay unhappily focused on negative behaviour for too long. Simply enjoy your child by being mindful of their presence.

Consider the following ideas to help with this process of mindfulness:

- Plan to be present with your child for a moment every day and think about how special that is for you. If you do this daily, it will start to become a habit and it will start positively changing how you process problems with them.

- Take photos and proudly display them. Reflect personally on each scene for a minute and enjoy that moment you shared together.

- Choose a special time of the day which you share together. This could be at bedtime, in the car, at mealtimes and so on. On these occasions, reflect on what your child is saying or doing; stop and listen deeply for a moment. Shut out the distractions around you and be present in that moment. Some parents like to write down their thoughts and it begins to form a journal of beautiful self-reflections on their child.

Laughter is a great experience to share. Try to find some time when you laugh together. One of my greatest fans was my grandmother. I have a lasting image of her dancing around the kitchen with a tea towel on her head. It is that image I remember when I think of her. It's a happy warm memory, a snapshot of a remarkable woman in my life.

There is an art in stopping movies in between scenes to process the images and feelings. Consider doing this with our daily experience. You're capturing moments on your emotional lens and savouring the scene. Don't press the play button too soon!

Memories are lasting

I often say to parents, 'Imagine what you would like your children to say about you at their twenty-first birthday or even your funeral!'

These children will grow up and reflect on the longer picture of their life's journey with their family, especially about how they were valued and heard. Think about your own memories of how you grew up. I'd imagine you'll have an image of how you were loved and how your parents nurtured you. The little details often get lost in the wash, but it's the general feeling of how your own parents loved and cared for you that counts.

Sometimes we become so focused on the small daily problems without considering that a child just sees you as the overarching person looking after their well-being. It's quite common in counselling students that they quickly refer to the general image they have of their parents. For example, 'Yes, mum understands me,' or 'I can talk to dad because he listens to me.' These images are being formed as they grow. They can sense how they're being cared for through their parent's overall manner with them.

'Patience', 'understanding', 'peacefulness' and 'sympathy' are words I often hear from children who talk about their families. When a child feels vulnerable around their parents – because they have been in trouble – their first anxiety is how they lose value in the eyes of their parents.

A great activity to do with children is to ask them to draw their family as animals and talk about their character through the image of the animals. For example, some may draw an owl as they see their parents as wise. Some may draw a zebra as mum as she is always running and on the go. This could be a fun activity for all the family. Always keep in mind the big picture. This is about the overall feeling a child has about how they're valued and nurtured.

Getting away from the maddening crowds

Busy families make for busy and noisy times and sometimes it's hard to find that special one-on-one time with children.

A family operates as a whole unit and how they talk to each other is often done as a group and not one-on-one. Too many interferences and interactions make it difficult to hear the individual cry of the child. If you're a second or a third child, you were born into a noisy family. Sometimes the simple design of the home can make for less chances to talk individually to children.

When I chat to parents who are struggling to identify with unacceptable behaviour, I make a very simple recommendation. Surprise them! Take them out of school for the afternoon and spend one-on-one time with them. Give them this unusual treat and it's surprising how they respond. You will be giving them some quality time together that's special for the two of you.

This approach I recommend often surprises parents, given my role as a principal. This special time gives them a sense of being heard. Invite them to suggest another way to find some special time together when it's needed.

What's to lose in one afternoon away from school?

Chapter 8

Being supportive

How to be helpful when a child is really upset

Think about yourself for a minute. When you're truly upset how much real listening occurs? Very little is the simple answer. No one listens to advice when feeling under pressure.

The same applies to children. When anxieties reach high levels, it's best to allow time for a child to calm down and to allow the high emotions to work through their system. Of course, younger children will go from zero to ten fairly quickly when upset. Once emotions cloud listening, there's no chance to talk through issues or to solve problems.

How do you help your child when they're upset? Here are some steps you can take:

- Ensure they're safe.
- Provide a quiet environment, if possible.
- Try not to interrupt them with reassurance until their upset feelings have reduced significantly.
- Be present and, in the case of a younger child, sometimes just holding them closely is comforting.

- Try not to interpret the behaviour too quickly. Just be present and calm when the emotions are high.
- If possible, try to eliminate other distractions such as other siblings talking or interfering, television, noise and so on. Sometimes dimming lights and creating a calming environment is helpful and quite soothing for an upset child.

When your child seems calmer, it might be possible to talk about what was so upsetting in the first place or sometimes it's best to leave it until later.

Simple reassurance is helpful. For example:

> *'Something has really upset you. When you're ready, I'm happy to talk to you about it.'*

This isn't a time to probe and question your upset child. There is sometimes residual anxiety that comes after being upset and children need time to recover and process their feelings. As a parent, there's no need to solve the problem and to make the child happy straightaway. A child's equilibrium will return after they feel better in themselves and move on.

Being upset and reacting to issues is a normal part of growing up. Children need to understand that expressing their feelings is acceptable. As adults, we tend to tailor our responses to anxiety quite differently, as we're conscious of other people, social pressures and different environments.

It's acceptable and natural as a parent to be upset from time to time and for your child to see your reaction to being upset. Again, this is modelling to your child that it's natural to be affected by issues and that adults need time to process issues too. What they observe is how you handle the anxiety and being upset and how you manage yourself. It's best to talk to your child about what can upset you and how you manage it. Hiding vulnerable emotions from your child only makes them anxious.

When children are very upset in the school setting, often a quiet space is found for them and no discussion is had until the child is in a calm state and ready to listen.

Giving real attention to your child

'Of course,' I hear you say, 'I give my child plenty of attention.'

Here I'll discuss some strategies on how to listen to a child in a deeper and more effective way.

Parents will naturally try to be available to their child as often as possible. However, giving real attention is more about how you present yourself when attending to your child. When working with children, it was common to hear them say that no one listens to them. When discussing this with parents they would be surprised and naturally reflect on how much time they gave their child.

So much of our parenting is done on the run!

Here are some suggestions of listening to a child in a deeper and more effective way:

- When your child wants to talk to you about something, decide if you have the time to stop and listen. If not then say,

'That's important to you.
I want to talk to you about that later.'

- When listening to your child, sit comfortably and give uninterrupted eye contact. This shows them that you're really paying attention. Take care not to jump into the conversation too quickly because this stops their flow of conversation and questions whether you're really listening to them.

- Often a child, especially a younger child, can talk too much but, waiting patiently will get you to the issue. Find a personal space in which to talk quietly so that you're not distracted.

- Don't do this process if you're not in the right frame of mind to listen. Delaying the conversation leads to better success later.

- Interject with affirming words, for example: 'hmm', 'keep going', 'that's interesting.' Such interjections encourage your child to keep talking because they believe that you're really listening and interested.

- If another child intervenes in the conversation, it's important to remind them that you're only talking to one person and that's important to you.

- Find a space that isn't too noisy. It's amazing how quiet spaces encourage listening.

- Never understate the importance of the child's conversation. Be consistent in your behaviour towards their conversations. If they believe you're a real listener, then be a listener.

- Once your child has disclosed what they want to say and you're ready to talk about it, affirm them for their efforts and acknowledge how you really enjoy listening to what they have to say. For example:

> *'You really told me what's on your mind, thanks for keeping me well informed.'*

These suggestions work well when you have the time. Keep in mind that effective listening is much more valuable than spending more time listening ineffectively and often 'on the run'. Your child demands less from you when they feel that real listening occurs.

Chapter 9

Strategies

Enjoying the process

Did you ever see the Australian film, *The Castle*?

The character of the father, Darryl Kerrigan, loved his wife's, Sal Kerrigan's, cooking. This was a wonderful example of affirming and celebrating the effort. Yes, I agree the story was exaggerated but nonetheless it highlighted how affirming people's efforts spurs them on to greater heights.

Children particularly respond to affirmation along the way. This means that we acknowledge their progress, rather than focussing on the end result.

For example:

> *'You've started your homework. Well done.'*

> *'I love the way you got up in time for school.'*

> *'Thanks for putting away your clothes. Well done.'*

It's all about celebrating the journey.

Applaud the small efforts, many of which we just take for granted. This gives your child the understanding that they're valued.

A great trick of mine is to always make some small affirmation when a child enters my office. This gives me some brownie points as the child feels appreciated. For example:

> *'Thanks for visiting me, I appreciate how you entered so quietly.'*

We're immediately on good footing – even if we need to talk about something serious.

This is all about demonstrating to your child that you value their efforts as well as teaching gratitude.

Learning to deal with conflict

We're always on the lookout for preventative measures to avoid conflict in our family setting. This is no doubt a sensible way of allowing a child to have a balanced childhood with appropriate affirmation, encouragement and reduced conflict. Having said this, a child will still need to develop skills in recognising and managing conflict. This starts very early in their life. At kindergarten, children begin to learn cooperative play by mixing with other children through sharing and group work. Some say that babies have very intense feelings from birth. They sense how their mother feels – especially when they're anxious.

Conflict is a natural part of life and, as children mature, skills need to be developed that enable them to better understand themselves and their ability to work effectively with others. They need to develop an awareness of their feelings and reactions to certain situations and to develop a language that enables them to cope with potential conflict in their day-to-day life. Some call this emotional competence.

A parent can help a child develop these competencies in the following ways:

- How you model social interactions is crucial to their developing an understanding of how to manage conflict. If a parent is overreactive, angry and nonreflective, this will impact on your child's understanding of managing conflict. If they see you attempt to remain calm, look at the situation clearly and resolve the matter through dialogue and negotiation, this instead has a very positive impact on them.
- Teaching your child how to negotiate is a key skill you're giving them in managing conflict. For example:

> *'I understand we have a problem with going to bed on time. Let's find ways to solve this problem together.'*

> *'I'm upset that you're not doing your chores. Let's list ways of helping you do them.'*

Teaching negotiation shows children that providing options will help solve the problem and will hopefully have an outcome of a win-win situation.

When a conflict occurs, remember this is a time to demonstrate modelling. Ensure you slow down, choose a good time to work through the issue with your child and definitely don't deal with the conflict on the run. Begin to look at how both you and your child can look at the issue working towards respecting each other's needs. This will involve compromise, and this is a wonderful emotional tool you, as a parent, can give to your child.

Schools are well set up when it comes to dealing with issues of conflict, especially given that student well-being coordinators are available to support students. Most schools teach a range of social skills in class as well as restorative justice, which helps children understand their own feelings and other's feelings in a conflict. Be in touch with your child's teachers when concerns about school are raised at home.

When working with children who were quick to temper and had not yet developed social skills to manage conflict, I would give them this four-step plan:

1. Stop and think.
2. What number on the angry scale would you give yourself?
3. If high, walk away, take big breaths and allow some time before dealing with the problem.
4. If you feel unsure about the skills to work through the problem, seek out an adult.

If we teach our children not to immediately react, often the level of anger drops down and the situation can be dealt without escalation.

'With our thoughts we make the world.'
– Buddha

Asking for help

As an adult, do you find it natural to ask for help or do you find asking questions about awkward situations difficult?

Often, we treat it as a natural process to ask for help. We're not embarrassed or feel uncomfortable. Of course, you can feel uncomfortable about asking for help but generally, as we get older, we show more maturity about asking difficult questions. It seems a normal thing to do.

Children need to acquire the skill of asking for help and questioning. If they acquire this skill from an early age it becomes a natural way of operating and is understood to be the best and the most natural response when you don't know the answer to any situation. I refer to its acquisition as a skill, so that we understand the very real value in asking questions and seeking help.

Some children, especially those that worry about making mistakes, can be reticent to ask for help. After all, does it suggest failure and a recognition to those around you that you don't know the answer?

What will people think of me?

Seeking help and asking questions should become a natural process of learning.

One of the most contemporary methods of teaching is the inquiry-based approach to learning, which is based around asking questions. In fact, the bigger the question, the better scope to learn. This tells us that asking questions is recognised as an important way of learning and living from day to day.

If you have a child reluctant to ask questions and to seek help when needed, the following suggestions may help encourage them:

- Talk to your child about how you like to ask questions to get more information. Highlight the time that seeking help solved your problem. For example:

    'Thank goodness I asked for directions on that trip. We would never have arrived on time without some assistance.'

    'I asked your teacher how I could help you with homework and she gave me some excellent ideas. Without her help, I would never know what to do.'

- Talk about important people who ask many questions to complete their work. For example, scientists and doctors are all professions that rely on gathering more information through questioning to help with their work.

- When a child talks about a problem, suggest some questions that they could ask to get the problem solved. For example:

    'You seem unsure about that homework. Let's think about some questions to get help from the teacher'.

Take these five examples:

1. 'When do you hand the homework to the teacher?'
2. 'What part of the homework is the most difficult?'
3. 'Is it better to spread the homework out over several days?'
4. 'Do you need more time to do this work?'
5. 'Which part of the homework is the easiest?

Bringing questions into play is all about breaking down the anxiety about the problem and ensuring that it's all manageable. Questioning and seeking help also is seen as a legitimate way of moving from not knowing to being informed.

When working with children who didn't like asking questions or seek help in the classroom, we would turn it into a game. I would ask a question about a set problem and they would respond. Then it was their turn to ask a question about the problem. We would see who could ask the most questions about the problem we set down and who gained the most information.

Affirming the child when they ask questions or seek help spontaneously is always a great tool used in the classroom. Try it at home:

'Well done, that question was a great one.'

'I'm so glad you asked me to help you.'

'I like that question. It's really got me thinking.'

Seeking help and asking questions should become a natural process of learning in which the child feels comfortable and invites others into their process of thinking. We also feel less anxious and less vulnerable when we seek help and question.

> *'The art of proposing a question must be held of higher value than solving it.'*
> – **Georg Cantor**

What time is the right time?

Choosing the right time of day makes all the difference for planned activities with your child. I would choose to work with children in a morning session as opposed to the afternoon because children are more retentive and receptive to what you have to say at that time. Their listening skills are much more responsive, they're less reactive to issues and can process at a calmer level. In a classroom setting, teachers are very aware that the more serious learning will be happening in the morning block and not the afternoon after children have eaten and played.

A lot of emotion comes into the afternoon – especially if play didn't provide a successful outcome. Often, activities provided in the afternoon in a classroom are shorter, require less focus and teachers set less expectation for their students.

If you're planning a special time with your child – such as a visit to the zoo, museum or visiting a friend – I recommend planning for the morning block. That way your child will be more attentive and their listening skills more attuned.

It sounds simple but if you want a quality experience from the activity or simply want a better response from your child, try morning blocks where possible.

Short, sharp breaks make all the difference

How much do we concentrate across the day?

In today's fast-moving world, where technology drives so much of the pace in which we live, it's not surprising when our concentration spans are reduced. Some put this down to technology and social media that demands instant response. We're also aware that children don't learn in the same way that generations before them did. They don't need to stretch their brain by learning large slabs of information when so much knowledge is available at their fingertips.

The changing face of how we process also suggests that concentrating for long periods of time is more difficult. Teachers are more aware of this and will plan lessons with regular and short breaks. Sometimes this will include some physical exercise to create space from the previous activity and to refresh thinking after some exercise. It works!

Now think about home. Sometimes tensions rise and this can happen when playing games together, watching television or doing homework. As a parent, we sometimes tend to react when the noise rises among siblings and other family members.

Consider being proactive by stopping the activity and propose some other option, such as calling time out and asking children to have quiet time in their room. It doesn't need to be for too long, it's simply about breaking the increasing tension.

When working with children who were highly anxious, it was common practice to change the environment in which we were working; sometimes we would go for a walk in the schoolyard or check out the preps. It was about creating a circuit breaker which shifted a child's focus to reduce tension.

This also applies to parents. Once our anxieties rise, we need to regulate them by creating space for ourselves to alleviate the pressure. It's amazing how a few minutes away from the problem can reduce tensions to a level where we can control our behaviour more rationally.

> 'Taking time to do nothing often brings everything into perspective.'
> **– Doe Zantamata**

Teach our children to like themselves first

A big issue for children at any age is to find a friend and sustaining friendships can be difficult for some children. Once a child feels vulnerable and struggles to settle into a friendship, they often manifest behaviour which can be quite unappealing to other children, generally in the form of attention seeking or sulking.

Once a child is at peace with themselves, they will naturally find it easier to make friends. Often, parents come up with all sorts of suggestions to their child about how to make a friend and most fail as the suggestions aren't able to be translated on the school yard.

For example, when you notice a strength of your child, talk about it. When you see them being joyous and happy, comment on how nice it is when they smile. Every time you notice how positive others are to your child, you might say:

'It looks like Jenny likes the way you pass the ball in basketball,'

or

'Did you notice how Josh smiles at you when you told that joke?'

Here you're simply encouraging them to reflect on their behaviour and the impact it has on others.

When working with children, I would sometimes encourage them to write down something they liked about another child. When the other child read what was written about them, it had quite an impact in recognising how they were valued.

Most children have to work at building friendships, slowly and steadily, and many go through the pain of losing them and having to re-establish themselves. This is quite normal and over time most develop strategies in building lasting relationships through trial and error.

As a parent, your role is to raise their awareness of how capable they are in various areas, especially social ones.

For example:

> *'I noticed how happy Jack was when you helped him with his Lego set.'*

As your child's self-confidence and emotional maturity grows, they will naturally attract friendships because they will learn the important rule that relationships work when you value the other person.

Lastly, never underestimate how they observe your relationships with friends. It's all about watch and learn from parents!

Keeping a happy journal that tells of success

Research tells us that using positive psychology with children is highly effective in building emotional stamina. Children will always grow from the positive in their life. How do we feel as adults when our boss gives us an affirmation? This is often a stimulus to feeling successful: 'someone values me!'

Keeping a positive journal is highly effective. This journal is a book where you write positive statements about your child. For example, 'Today I loved the way you smiled at me'. This book then becomes a collection of positive memories. Simple concepts are all that is needed.

I recommend no more than one thought a day or even a few statements across the week. Children love going back over the book and reading the positive comments. This is especially helpful when they're having a less happy time.

In counselling, we would call this narrative therapy, where we recognise that the written word is valuable. I've used this method quite often in school and also with my staff. Just imagine how we feel when we receive beautiful thoughts on a birthday card. This is similar to receiving a birthday card, but more often. And how many birthday cards do we keep over the years?

Building a picture of success

Never underestimate the value of simple sticker charts. These can be set up on the fridge at home or anywhere visible to the family. When a child receives a sticker, it indicates that they're achieving success in a goal that you're setting.

Remember, keep the goal simple and set up the environment for your child to be successful. A simple coloured sticker goes a long way with children. This happy chart reminds them that they're capable of being successful and is especially effective with younger children. They also love the visual impact, especially when they see the stickers building in number.

Talking about the growth on the chart is also affirming their ongoing success.

A few tips with sticker charts:

- Keep the goal simple. Let them achieve their goal perhaps after a few stickers as children struggle with long-term goals. Celebrate at the end with some agreed rewards. Occasionally mention how successful they were in achieving those goals.

- Children in primary settings are very familiar with setting goals and so this habit will be consistent with how teachers work at school. It's common that at parent-teacher chats, children will talk about the goals they set in class and how they're working towards achieving them.

It's all about building a healthy process in being successful.

A quick anger buster

Let's break through that quick anger!

Some children can be calm one moment and then without any understanding of what has actually happened, their mood can go from zero to ten. It can be explosive and frustrating to understand as a parent.

Parents find this difficult to manage given that the behaviour comes from an unknown source. But the first thing to understand is that when a child is highly emotive, their reasoning and ability to listen and respond to logic won't be present. Therefore, rationalising won't work. It's best to wait for a time when your child is calmer. For example, you could say:

> *'I'm very unhappy when you get angry quickly.'*

How do you break through your child's anger? If your child is then able to tell you what the anger was about, follow with:

> *'When you have those feelings again, tell me and together we can work it out.'*

Ask them to give you a number from one to ten as to how they're feeling. This makes it easy for them to explain their frustration level.

Sometimes instant anger occurs because your child's language isn't developed enough to respond to the situation with effect. Teach your child that expressing feelings through language is a great way to let you know how they feel.

For example, teach them that they can say:

'I'm angry because ...'

'I'm sad because ...'

'I feel unhappy when ...'

'I'm frightened when ...'

Expressing emotions out loud actually starts the process of feeling better.

Sometimes having a feelings chart at home can help with younger children. I use it all the time to start conversations about feelings and I've noticed that children actually look for the chart to start the conversation.

Another way to help is to write down some feeling words and put them around the house. Your child could decorate the words and discuss them with you before they're placed in a noticeable area in the house. Invite them to use these words when feeling unsettled.

Getting feelings out in the open starts the healing process.

Taking on something new

What a great idea! Here I refer to stepping out of your comfort zones and into a whole new field. How often do we do this in our busy routines? I imagine not too often given the demands on our weeks and the expectations placed on us in many different ways. Who wants to put themselves through such an ordeal?

Research tells us that we create new pathways in our brain by stretching our thinking processes into completely new areas and this is great for our children. However, remember that routine is important, and children need repetition and opportunities to reinforce much of what they do and learn.

But, as parents, we need to demonstrate to our children that reaching out and trying new and different experiences is a way of life. It fuels our appetite for change and ignites our interest in the broader world.

As we age, it's comfortable for us to continue with what we know and enjoy in our lives. Familiarity is certainly predictable. While this has its place, I would also suggest taking a few risks and demonstrating to your child that risk-taking and seeking out new ways of being and doing are very rewarding.

Stepping outside of your comfort zone is great for your kids. Consider the following pointers on how to encourage your child to be hungry for new experiences:

- Remember that you're the significant model in this situation. If you demonstrate to your child that you enjoy taking on new ideas in your life, this will have a major impact on your child.
- Talk positively about taking a few risks, trying on new ideas and talk about situations where risk-taking changed your thinking.

- When you notice your child steering away from the regular routine, affirm their efforts. For example:

  'Well done. I just noticed that you chose a different way of working out that sum. That shows initiative.'

  'I really like the way you tried to put your Lego together. Trying new ways can lead to different shapes.'

  'I love the new outfit you're wearing. It has a different look from your regular clothes.'

- When working through a problem with your child, suggest brainstorming different ways of handling it.
- When you take on a new direction, talk to your child about what's new and different about this step and why you chose to try it. For example:

  'I think when I go to work tomorrow, I'll try a new route. The traffic is just too heavy at the moment.'

- Be bold and specific in making suggestions to the family that take them out of their comfort zones. For example:

  'Let's eat Japanese tonight! We've never had it before, and it could be a delicious and fun experience.'

- Show your child that you value attempting new and different experiences and that you include them in this process.
- With taking on something new, it also helps cope with fear of failure. For example:

> *'I'm starting to learn Italian. It may take some time and practice as I'll make mistakes along the way.'*

Set up a climate in the family where new experiences are seen as a positive because it encourages new ways of being and doing.

> *'Never be afraid to try something new because life gets boring when you stay within the limits of what you already know.'*
> **– Kylie Francis**

Developing independence early

We invite our children to take small steps to independence as they grow, and this will become a way of life for both of you. The more children work towards being independent, the greater capabilities they develop intellectually, socially, emotionally and physically. This means a reduction of control for you, but, in another way, you're teaching your child how to be a capable and independent soul.

We can't be in the presence of our children exerting control all the time. We also shouldn't aim to attend to every detail in our children's lives to ensure that we're managing everything just the way we like it. Gradual injecting of independence into your child is all about building a strong and confident young individual who likes themselves enough to take up opportunities, shows creativity and lives with emotional stamina.

Teachers give children small, incremental opportunities to facilitate independence. This can happen through work demands or social demands. When a child shows initiative of a new nature – let's say a little riskier – a teacher will encourage the child to keep going in this new area. Teachers will also recognise very quickly in their classroom those children who come from a home where the child is encouraged to take on new challenges and to show independence in family activities.

By giving your child incremental bouts of being independent, you're saying to your child that you trust them. Total control demonstrates having no faith in a child's abilities.

Gradually letting your child become independent shows that you're expecting them to take a dive from time to time. This is natural and this is where your talents and skills come into the story. You're there to listen, recommend options and dust them down when they're feeling bruised and sore from their fall. Afterall, every childhood has its ups and downs.

You're there to also affirm their efforts and talk about how they showed initiative in 'having a go' on their own. This is a helpful and useful role to take on and a much more effective position as a parent. Trying to solve everything for them where a child does no independent thinking and takes no ownership of problems delays their emotional growth. In fact, they don't even see problems because they're taken away from them.

Here are some tips on becoming a more relaxed parent and slowly giving your child independence:

- Firstly, notice your child's strengths. These are good starters for giving some more independence to your child:

  'I can see how well you fold clothes. Could you fold those clothes on the bench for me? Thanks.'

  'I like the way you manage money. Could you pay the cashier with this money? Thank you.'

- Gradually take stock of areas in which your child is less secure and begin building some support for their confidence in acting independently. For example:

  'Rather than me explaining to the teacher why you were away today, I would like you to tell her when we go to school tomorrow.'

This will help a shy child articulate themselves to their teacher.

- When your child has genuinely 'had a go' and continues to be unsuccessful, sit down together and write down optional ways to 'have a go.' At no point do you take over the problem completely.
- As a family, talk about family activities or routines where jobs can be shared. Were the jobs a good distribution for all family members? Were some jobs too much? Do you need to redefine the jobs? Are there more difficult jobs now to share?

When working with children who were dealing with some issues, it was important to listen to their attempts in solving the problem. Without that component in the discussion, it would not be a joint discussion through facilitation, rather, it would be instructional.

Teach your child to develop staying power

So much of this modern technologically driven world is all about fast moving, immediate satisfaction and moving on quickly. Sometimes this can flow into other aspects of a child's life where they actually need to find grit and sustain the effort. It's easy to say, 'This doesn't suit me, so I'll just move on to something else less arduous with quick success.' However, perseverance is key and involves a child learning to keep on trying, having a go and showing determination to achieve a task.

As a parent, it's valuable to talk about how rewarding it is to persevere and how carrying it through its stages is the key for success. How often do our children see the value of 'having a go' and being consistent in their efforts to achieve a tricky goal? The more we encourage them to stay motivated to achieve difficult tasks, the better they grow in valuing their own capabilities.

I appreciate that this isn't easy, but there are several strategies you can teach them to keep up the staying power:

- Talk about the endurance you sometimes need to complete a task. For example, have you started going to the gym and find it difficult, but you're determined to keep going to reap the benefits?

- Perhaps you're studying at university; talk about the rigour and effort you need to put into getting better. No pain, no gain.

- Talk about the success you personally feel when you go through the trial and error of working at something.

- If your child is involved in recreational activities – such as sport, dancing or the drama club – they must recognise the effort to get better or increase fitness, where performance can be quite demanding. Ask them how they feel after they succeed.

- Set simple goals with your child. For example:

> *'I know you're keen to get better at maths. Let's put an extra twenty minutes into learning maths at the end of every day.'*

Once goals are set and achieved, talk about the process and how putting in effort had successful outcomes.

When working with children who were reluctant to push themselves, we would start by talking about successful people they knew, especially their heroes. We talked about how they became successful and focused on the great efforts and sacrifices they made to achieve their goals. We then talked about simple tasks that the children had achieved with some effort; it was about building on small strengths.

Teachers are very skilled at this; they affirm regularly and celebrate when children take that extra leap. For a parent, they must be alert to any staying power that their child demonstrates and then affirming their effort. Keep in mind here that we're not always affirming the result, but the progressive effort and endurance shown by the child. For example:

> *'Great effort. So, do you think that in a week you will be able to improve on your spelling test? What will you do to achieve this goal?'*

Helping your child increase their staying power is about strengthening their self-resolve.

> *'It always seems impossible until it's done.'*
> **– Nelson Mandela**

Giving your child tools to defend themselves

It's hard work sticking up for yourself as a little one in the schoolyard. The following is about teaching your child, or a child in your care, some simple 'I' statements that give them a sense of control that don't lead to unnecessary conflict.

Sit with your child and talk about the feelings they have when things go wrong. They will likely come up with feelings of anger, upset, unhappy or frightened.

Then teach them how to use those words when feeling unsettled in any situation.

For example:

> *'I'm unhappy when you hit me.'*

> *'I'm angry when you take my book.'*

> *'I'm frightened when you shout at me.'*

You're teaching them to use the 'I' followed by the feeling they have and the act that upsets them.

Practice this at home in any situation that might occur between siblings. When you see your child upset firstly find out what negative emotions they're experiencing and then discuss how to express it with an 'I' statement.

By teaching them to express their feelings about someone else's behaviour you're giving them tools to manage their problems. This is a very healthy way for them to express their frustrations and it gives them more ownership of their uncomfortable emotions.

Of course, practice is necessary, but once a child sees the value and feels successful, they will begin to automatically use this technique. A child who has confidence and has language skills that are strong and effective will have the best tools to manage difficult conversations.

Learning how to live without ownership of everything

What a difficult lesson it is to teach our children that we don't need to own everything. This is tricky, especially when so many other children around them seem to have so much more than they do.

> *'Strive to have access to things. Not ownership of them.
> Possess something and it possesses you.'*
> **– Linus Mundy**

This quote touches on family values and how a child understands what's possible and not possible in their family setting. It's about teaching your child that we live within our means.

In my experience, families that play together, laugh together, talk together, physically exercise together and so on, demonstrate to their children that there are many ways to access things but not own them. The more motivated they are with regard to accessing what is available for them, the greater appreciation they develop for what is around.

Families can also talk about their finances and what constitutes living within their means. This is a worthwhile life lesson to teach children. In today's world, where financial transactions take place with credit cards, children usually don't get a visual understanding of cost.

Here are some useful tips:

- Set limits with the whole family and discuss how the family budget works – perhaps across a week. It's best to keep it short and in simple terms. It's about getting the child to reflect on the cost of living.
- Celebrate all the opportunities where the family can access things as opposed to owning them. For example, as mentioned above, utilising all the natural resources available in the area.

- Encourage your child to research the price of items. This is great for their maths, but also gets them to understand the value of goods.
- If a child has pocket money, then teach them to save for something special, this will give them pleasure in their efforts. Grandparents can be a great support in quickly building up their resources.
- As a family, budget for one special item and tap into how saving money is going over time.
- Birthdays or Christmas are a great occasion for a child to receive something special. Waiting until the occasion has arrived teaches the lesson of patience as well as placing more value on the gift.
- Encourage your child to write thank you cards when given something special. This helps them reflect on the giver's thought and effort.
- Tell stories of your childhood and the excitement of waiting for gifts – perhaps you had a paper round or worked to earn small amounts of money. Talk about the joy you felt when the effort was rewarded.
- If the answer is 'no' to something they want, be prepared to explain the reason and listen to their concerns. Can you negotiate with them or is it simply not within budget expectations?
- Keep coins at the ready in your purse or wallet and invite your child to count out and pay for items with coins.

I've had the privilege of managing schools in different economic zones. What I learned was that those children with less seem to appreciate what they received with gratitude and developed a deeper understanding of its value. They also displayed considerable creativity in their play. For our children in more affluent areas, appreciation and gratitude can be harder lessons to learn in some cases. Families are highly influential in this area.

If a family demonstrates restraint and self-management, this is a lesson well taught to a child. Finding happiness isn't in the material things in life.

Crazy and creative ideas for long stays at home

I've been giving this some thought and I want to tell you a story that may develop some ideas. Many years ago, as a young teacher and very interested in developing the creative side to my class, my students and I all decided to turn the classroom into a pirate ship. We had been reading an adventure book on pirates which captured the children's imagination. We also listened to the operetta, 'Pirates of Penzance'.

This was an extraordinary adventure. We took at least one week to build the ship and surrounds. We researched what an old ship would look like and found all sorts of pieces to put it together. Desks were removed from the classroom and the whole room became the ship. Much to the displeasure of the principal, we were determined to keep this room alive and for the next few weeks we learned all about the ship, how winds moved and influenced sailing. We learned about tides and wrote poetry. It was an incredible adventure of building a slow steady piece of art from which we had so much enjoyment and learning. Years later, I met up with students who still remembered the experience. This became a powerful learning tool.

Consider doing something quite innovative at home. Given the length of time you have on holidays, let your house become the creative space. How about setting up a room which can be converted into something creative where the children can experience play and learning? Perhaps a games room?

Invite the children into brainstorming what that room could look like and using all sorts of scraps and ready materials. Be generous enough to let them experiment.

Also consider painting a room. Under instruction, a child can assist.

The garden is an extraordinarily creative space. How about the children make an art piece for the garden? This could take some time, perhaps several days. The joy is in the process. How about painting the rocks or setting up a chicken coop?

Of course, cooking – especially baking – is a wonderful creative exercise for children. Consider it hospitality 101 at home.

Are there arts and crafts you can teach your child such as knitting or sewing? I hear macramé is back in fashion. Check out places like art and craft shops, junk yards and op shops that can offer cheap supplies for art and craft activities.

I've recently heard of a dad building a bike with his children using old parts.

Do you have old bikes or toys that could be used for the creation of an art piece? Children love pulling apart old equipment.

If your home will be your total sanctuary for several weeks, set it up to accommodate movement and space for the children. Remove objects that will create stress when damaged. This is important for your sanity. Accept that for a few weeks the home will be a different space in which to live. It will be a space for active living.

Can you build a cubby house or go carts with your children? It's all about doing activities that require a focus, time and patience.

How about technology? Look online for some short courses that are enjoyable and have a learning aspect to them. Of course, watch and monitor screen time.

How about making home videos or writing songs?

Children thrive on being creative and if you create a home environment that enables them to express themselves, they can entertain themselves in unique and intuitive ways over longer sustained periods.

'Creativity is contagious. Pass it on.'
– Albert Einstein

Chapter 10

A child's brain

Is your child developing a growth mindset?

The best and most positive way to go forward with your child is to develop a growth mindset and not a fixed mindset. A growth mindset is about looking at situations and seeing how it can be understood from a position that will lead to growth and new understandings.

The growth of capabilities is all about how you manage it. As a parent, you should encourage your child to see situations as positive opportunities rather than having a fixed and negative outlook. An example of a fixed outlook is if a child comes home from school and talks about how they didn't play well at lunchtime with their friends and so they won't play with them again – after all, they feel better to avoid failure. This is definitely a fixed mindset. Rather, we should encourage our children to consider talking to their friends about the game or perhaps playing a different game with them. Whatever the discussion, it's about not seeing the incident as failure but an opportunity for growth.

We can help develop in our children, the idea that we learn from anything we do. You could say:

> *'Sounds like you need to talk to your friends about games that work for everyone.'*

Frequently talking this way about incidents that haven't gone well teaches your child that there are many ways at looking at situations. The best way forward can be to use a failed situation to improve yourself. For example:

> *'You seem upset that the test didn't go well. How about talking to the teacher about what went wrong so that you can get better at that problem?'*

Here you're reflecting on the fixed outcome and turning it into an opportunity. Another example:

> *'Oh dear, the sandcastle fell down. Let's look in the bucket to see how we can make a better one.'*

When working with children that felt unsuccessful and would give up easily, teachers would often invite them to set small goals or simply lay out in front of them different ways to see the problem. This was all about looking at re-framing the issue.

When I worked with children who seemed to have a fixed mindset about situations, we would discuss all the positive things that could be derived from the situation. We would often list them and discuss what we learnt from them.

For example:

> *'You seem so unhappy that you can't spell very well. Let's look at the words you got correct that shows that you can spell.'*

This teaches children the idea that we learn from anything we do, and this especially includes when things go wrong. These occasions give us a chance to continue to get better. It's all about finding hope in every situation if you look hard enough.

Do *you* have a fixed or a growth mindset?

Have you ever noticed that you sound like your parents when talking to your child? Or perhaps you work hard to parent very differently from your parents? Whatever your style, consider developing a growth mindset in engaging with your child because in order to teach your children to have a growth mindset, you must also have one yourself.

A growth mindset is about being open to ideas that your child might suggest that aren't consistent with how you normally operate. It can be trying new things that are different or just experimental moments as a family. It's about accepting that mistakes occur and that it takes time, effort and some risks to move forward.

On the other hand, a fixed mindset is about being reserved and not keen to take risks of any kind. It's about taking the predictable and certain route forward. It's about being safe and certain with regard to the outcomes.

Your child will keep providing challenges for you and it's worth reflecting on what kind of a mindset you give to their suggestions. When working with children it wasn't uncommon to hear them say:

'It won't work in my home,'

or

'It's not worth talking about that idea to mum.'

This suggests that they understand the fixed mindset of their parents and that ideas and suggestions aren't to be brought forward at home. I suggest keeping an open model at home that encourages varied conversations and applauds new ideas and initiatives that may be worth exploring or at least discussing.

I also suggest inviting your child to come up with suggestions for working through family matters. You could, for example, say things such as:

'I really love new ideas.'

'Sometimes it's great doing things differently.'

'Have you got some other ideas that might help?'

Our children are growing up in a world where developing a growth mindset will give them the confidence to experiment, show initiative and fit into a very flexible world where predictability might not be the order of the day.

By including your child in family discussions and brainstorming, you're being consistent with how children learn at school. Here children are encouraged to ask questions, try out ideas and explore options. This is how they learn best.

So, consider the following:

- Be open to their suggestions.
- Keep an open mind on what they have to say.
- Encourage creativity.
- Applaud the effort and process, not so much the result.
- Reward the interest in independent learning and thinking.

Does your child overthink?

Children vary so much in how they process information. Some children overthink issues by looking at all the possibilities and where it can go wrong, and this can build anxiety. Mentally, they measure out the situation in their mind and are reticent to put themselves forward. They look for the negatives in a situation and become too concerned about the risk and potential fear related to the challenge.

On the other hand, there are some children who simply plough ahead and don't reflect on risk or outcomes at all. These children are often easier going, more carefree and take more risks. However, for our overthinkers, life can be a little trickier as they negotiate their way through the maze of school, home pressures, friendship groups and so on.

Here are a few suggestions to help your overthinkers:

- If your child looks worried or seems to be processing information slowly try saying:

  'What positives have you just heard?'

  'How can we make this a simple thought?'

- When you see your child overthinking, break it up for them. For example:

  'Okay, so you have a test. Let's talk about that.'

  'What part of the test is on your mind?'

Talk positively about issues that can lead to overthinking. Ensure that your tone and your words convey optimism and hope.

When working with children, I would often invite an overthinking child to write down what was on their mind and together we would break it up into possibilities. This helped them learn to cope with situations that at first seemed too difficult. Getting them to repeat back what was on their mind made it easier to break up their concerns into possibilities.

Sometimes overthinkers are worried about being right or anxious about making errors. What we need to do is to remind them that we reward effort, not necessarily the outcome. For example:

'You seem to be thinking a lot about the race tomorrow.'

'Well done for having a go and working through what's on your mind. Let's talk about the concerns you have for tomorrow.'

The idea here is to teach them that overthinking can lead to too much worry and unnecessary complication. It's best to look at situations in a simple way that shows all the positive possibilities.

Are you being a builder or a blamer?

Are you more inclined to find out what and who caused the problem or do you recognise the problem as an opportunity to build on and strengthen a child's knowledge and relationship with you?

There are definitely two ways to see the situation and I invite you to reflect on how you approach a problem that you may be having with your child. Sometimes, it is difficult to find the positive in difficult situations but this article is encouraging you to be a builder and not so much the blamer. When we blame, we are looking for accountability and guilt? It can be a damning situation for a child when they feel that blame is all that is the focus. With blame comes being judgemental and downing the person. The person being blamed can feel shame and remorse. There are no positive feelings if blame is just given without any understanding.

However, it is possible to understand the problem, be aware of who is responsible and still work to improve changes. It is about reacting well and dealing with something positively. There will be lessons to learn and an opportunity to move on.

> *'I understand that you broke the glass.*
> *Let's look at how we can avoid that situation*
> *from happening again.'*

Here you acknowledge that there has been some accountability and that you can move on with a positive plan for the future. It is about using an incident and putting structures in place to ensure that it doesn't happen again. This takes away the heavy sense of blame and guilt and puts in place some positive reminders that doing something positive has better emotional outcomes. It is more about taking charge of the situation rather than becoming absorbed or fixated into the error of the deed.

Consider these ideas:
- Check in with yourself to find out if you are more inclined to blame when something happens.
- Are you a person who is quick to react? This can lead to blaming very quickly.
- Think about yourself as a proactive person. Can you see more of the solution rather than the problem when it happens? Can you learn to see the problem as an opportunity? It may mean reducing some of the initial angry response which can happen when an incident occurs.

Children who are used to being blamed can easily learn to avoid being honest. We all become anxious when we are around people who are quick to judge and blame.

A child will respect being honest as important if they are dealing with an adult that is fair and looks to solving problems rather than being quick to temper and blame.

'When you blame others, you give up your power to change.'
-Dr. Robert Anthony

Knowledge is Power

When we were in the grip of the lockdown, we were all seeking updates and new information with regard to the pandemic. Such knowledge was critical in keeping abreast of the situation that was at times quite confusing and unsettling. Managing anxiety and above all supporting the family through those uncertain times was the order of the day. Knowledge enabled us to take control of our daily life.

This is a classic example of how accurate knowledge gives you the power to manage and control the situation.

Children deserve accurate and up to date knowledge that will empower them to take control of their lives. As a parent, it is our duty to ensure that we are honest and give our children the knowledge that will empower them over all sorts of life matters. As a child grows, a parent of course tailor's information that fits the age but above all it must be the truth.

Teachers' roles are very much about empowering children with knowledge. They give them the tools to take control of their work. There is nothing more disempowering and limiting than not having the correct knowledge to drive decisions. It is like a ship lost in a storm with no anchor or guiding instruments to direct it.

Children trust their teachers because they will teach them accurately and with no holds barred. Teachers will be honest and empower them with useful knowledge. The more knowledge our children have, the greater power they have in taking control of themselves and being personally confident to tackle issues. We are all rendered powerless without knowledge.

Consider the following to help children in this area:

- When a child asks a question be in the habit of answering correctly and with information that is accurate. Underplaying your child's intelligence by offering simple answers can sometimes confuse a child. It can also suggest to the child that you do not have confidence in their ability to process information. This can reduce their interest in coming to you for knowledge.

- Children display their curiosity in many ways. We should be available and willing to answer questions that enlighten and empower your child. Let them know that you are happy to share knowledge together. If you don't have the answer straight away then follow up learning can happen together.

- Be consistent in how you answer questions. Check in with your child later to see if they understand what you had to say.

- Be prepared to learn from your child. There is much to discover from listening to them and respecting their knowledge.

- As a parent remember that the more you empower your child with knowledge, the better equipped they are in coping with various life situations. They are also more inclined to approach you with difficult issues if they feel you will give them an honest and rich explanation. This is particularly the case as the child approaches puberty.

- If you are a person who displays an insatiable appetite for knowledge, this will undoubtedly rub off on your child. Share your information and joy of learning with them.

- Be open to talking about all sorts of topics that sometimes may take you out of your comfort zones. Let your child know that exploring various topics can lead to stronger awareness and sensitivity to all kinds of differences. We are only intimidated by what we don't know.

A child who feels comfortable approaching a parent with all sorts of inquiries will undoubtedly feel comfortable and secure in your presence. They deserve the respect of being given accurate and clear information.

A child who values knowledge grows in the power of personal confidence and self-worth.

> *'An investment in*
> *KNOWLEDGE*
> *Always pays the best*
> *INTEREST'*
> **-Ben Franklin**

How to learn about patience

This is a tricky one for children. By nature, they are slow to be patient especially when they are young. They are living in a fast pace world where social media teaches them that instant gratification and immediate response is to be expected and highly valued. One could say that learning patience is an outdated skill. Consider even simple things. For example, do we wait to have hot cross buns at Easter? No, we find them in the shops as early as February when the last dying embers of Christmas are present.

We live in a world where instant satisfaction is expected and is regarded as the norm. It is not seen as impatience but a necessary requirement of daily life. It is all about we have a right to be happy all the time because we deserve getting what we want.

Teaching patience therefore is necessary as it does not come as an innate skill. People who work hard at being patient learn the art of waiting and with it the appropriate rewards. With patience comes a sense of being at peace and controlling the stress of having things straight away.

Fortunately, school teaches about the value of patience and accordingly rewards children for demonstrating an ability to be patient. Walk into any classroom and you will see many signs referring to dates when certain activities and celebrations will occur. There is often an excitable countdown to a special day. Children must wait for their name to be called out and at times may not be chosen straight away for activities. They have to go with the flow and learn the art of patience. And so, the list of reasons why patience is needed and demanded is clear in a school setting.

At home there are many occasions when patience can be encouraged as a great gift and is highly valued in your family. Waiting for a birthday is a typical one. The anticipation builds and then the excitement of the day. The wait is over and accordingly rewarded.

Consider:

- Can you think of several occasions across the week, month etc. when you can reinforce and reward a child's patience?
- Put up calendar dates on the fridge that you are looking forward to. Talk about the wait and the anticipation that is building.
- Do you know and admire patient people? Talk about them to your child. How were they rewarded? What made them so likeable?
- Ask your child about the times they had to be patient in their school day. Note how being patient kept the class moving.
- Demonstrate patience to your child in your own life.

> *"I have an important meeting with my boss this week. I will wait patiently for this as I think it is about my promotion."*

- How about the general nature of being patient? We wait to be served in a restaurant or perhaps we are in a queue at the supermarket. There are many daily occasions when patience is needed. These are perfect times to show your child that being patient is the best way forward. Impatience only leads to stress and poor behaviour on occasions.

Slowly and steadily, you can demonstrate and highlight times when patience wins the day. A child needs positive examples, especially as the anxiousness of society demands quick and immediate responses.

> *'We could never learn to be brave and patient, if there were only joy in the world.'*
> **-Helen Keller**

Teaching children the value of finishing

In our busy world there are some aspects of our work which may never get finished, however teaching our children that completing tasks, finishing agreed goals is a very satisfying and important way of being.

To value finishing a task, etc. is to have the maturity to know that completion is satisfying and healthy.

Children are busy little bees who can start activities and walk away from them quite easily. This is partly due to their age, span of concentration and shifting interests. No matter what age, we can teach them slowly the art and grace of finishing.

Teachers know how important it is to teach children to complete their tasks in class. They will plan to allow enough time or will make optional ways for a child to finish their work. It is all about the importance of actually finishing. As children grow older, they are taught that their performance at school will also be judged on their ability to complete tasks. So, from an early age working towards completing tasks, projects etc.

is considered a valuable tool in learning. Incomplete work is considered poor performance.

We can teach our children the importance of finishing by our own actions. Consider:

- When you complete a task talk about how it feels to have it finished.

> *'I feel so glad that I finished mowing the lawn. It is a job well done.'*

- Affirm your child when they demonstrate that they have finished tasks.

> *'Well done. Your homework is complete now. You still have some free time before dinner.'*

- Draw up a list of tasks to do for the week. Tick them off when complete. Show your child how much satisfaction you gain from ticking off that list. Each item ticked off is a job behind you.
- Encourage your child to come back to tasks incomplete. Remind them that no matter how much time is needed, the completion is all about being successful.

> *'You have taken some time to clean up your Lego on the floor, but now it is all complete. Well done. The floor is so tidy.'*

- Remind your child that there is no satisfaction in not finishing. The joy comes from completing the task and then comfortably moving on.
- Talk about some aspect of your work that gave you satisfaction once it was completed. Highlight the satisfied feeling you gained from completion. Also, what changed or grew as a result of completing the work?

Teaching your child, the satisfaction of finishing teaches them to appreciate and look forward to moving on. New horizons are born from completing tasks.

> *'If you're brave enough to start, you're strong enough to finish.'*
> **-Gary Ryan Blair**

Judging people can have a powerful influence on our children

Are we prone to making quick judgements of people? I would add, are we very vocal about our observations of others? The delicate question that I raise here is how much do we influence our children on the judgements we make of others.

It is natural to have opinions and often this comes from a life lived with increasing knowledge around and about people. If we find ourselves quite opiniated about people, are we in full possession of the facts? Young eyes and ears are around and it is not difficult for your judgements to become their judgements. After all at an early age they trust your opinions.

What in fact is life giving for our children is to be open to all kinds of people and to look for the best and not the worst of people. Having such a disposition is very attractive to others and is encouraging a more peaceful, mature way of being.

At school, teachers can see how influenced children become of others from the images formed by their parents. Once a child has such an attitude, they are working from the negative and not the positive.

A classroom is an excellent setting to teach children about accepting differences and growing to like the difference.

Consider:

- Take care with what is said about others in the presence of your child. You may have strong opinions about someone but I think it best to be subtle and careful in expressing them in front of your child. Let them slowly and gently form images of others for themselves.

- Encourage an attitude that everyone is different and I may have some thoughts about this situation or person but there are many opinions to be considered.

- Encourage your child to have an open mind when they encounter people with different views or perhaps ways of communicating.

- Teach them that having an opinion is natural but making judgements that damage can be harmful and lasting. Once judgements are made, opinions are sealed and limited understanding comes from making a judgement.

- If your child talks about a child in their class negatively discuss if they can see the good in that child and encourage them to be open to learning more about that person. A closed mind at an early age is not a healthy way to grow mentally and emotionally.

Social media sadly encourages judgment in all sorts of areas to do with people. Monitor what your child watches and have an open outlook on opinions and attitude about others. Teach them to be open to differences and to find some positive in difficult discussions about people that are controversial.

Developing the habit of making quick judgements on people can become a life habit. It closes doors mentally and disengages from learning more about people.

'If you judge people, you have no time to love them'.
-Mother Theresa

PART 2

Families

Chapter 11

Children and their families

The changing nature of families

Just when you think everything in your family is cosy and going well, along comes change. Yes, it's true: the nature of families continues to evolve and change as you and your children experience normal life experiences, and as the children grow. At school, it was common for parents to ask how their beautiful, innocent child – who had demonstrated sweetness and light – suddenly became difficult.

Young parents sending their first child to school were always surprised at the changes their child was making in their first year. Suddenly, the child's exposure to so many other influences loomed loud in their life.

As a family, there are certain factors that drive a healthy life across all the age periods that the child and family will experience. Nothing remains constant. Families will experience changes for a variety of reasons, and they will influence your child's response. For example, you may go back to work after being at home for some time or a crisis – perhaps a death or illness – can have a big impact on how a family operates and how they feel. As a family, there could be a crisis which causes major changes in the life of everyone: schools can change, teachers can suddenly move schools, and this destabilises your child's feeling of being secure.

Firstly, accept that change is inevitable and that you should welcome the change and various aspects of growth that you notice in your child. This may mean accepting some differences that challenge you as well. Let's look at some stable aspects to a family that will help us weather the storm as our family evolves over the years:

- As a family, have open communication and discuss how you welcome talking about changing ideas, beliefs and values that your child is coming across.
- Children become quite sensitive about their friends. Welcome all types into your home. This reassures your child that you value their judgement.
- Compliment them on their growing awareness of life. Sometimes children become anxious to express a different opinion in the house.
- Welcome and invite different opinions from your children. This leads to healthy, open discussion. Merely enforcing your values only limits the conversation.
- If and when something of a major nature occurs in the family, be open and honest with your child. Of course, providing age-appropriate information is necessary. However, your child needs to feel included when the family is going through a crisis and needs to have an honest understanding of what has happened that may impact their lives.

- It's important for a child to feel that their opinion matters. When they discuss new topics, which can cause you to have some concerns, be authentic in your response and genuinely interested in what they have to say. It's valuable to talk as a family about what drives all of you. In this way, children have reinforced ideas about what makes their family tick. They accept and enjoy its uniqueness.

When working with children, I was impressed with the emotional maturity of children who felt comfortable in open and honest discussions with their parents. They would choose their parents as the first port of call when they had a problem. They also had no reservation in talking about unsettling topics given that they knew their parents would be receptive to their discussion and value their thoughts.

Families are a living, breathing organism that needs regular emotional nourishment from within. The family continues to be nourished by healthy discussion and the ability of all members, no matter what age, to feel valued and credible as part of the group.

'To improve is to change, to be perfect is to change often.'
– Winston Churchill

Different generations

Each new generation has their unique challenges.

Our children are growing up in a different generation and will develop and grow subject to the development of that culture. This is natural. What I'm suggesting is to be a parental model that introduces a strong presence of compassion, empathy and gratitude into their life.

The more children live in the presence of such values, the more they are inclined to use them in their own experiences. The more they see their parents utilising these values in their own lives with others and themselves, the more they exhibit what has been modelled to them.

Here are some positive ways to present those virtues in your child's life:

- Talk openly about kind acts that you notice around you. Compliment your child when they demonstrate thoughtfulness to others. Encourage them to look for the generous spirit of others. For example:

> *'I was so impressed when I saw how your friend shared his toys.'*

- Many of the movies you watch together as a family often carry messages about humility and gratefulness. Talk about these virtues as a family. You can also teach a great deal through reading books together.
- When you're working through problems with your child, consider how you're communicating with them by being compassionate.
- Do you become overwhelmed by an issue or do you discuss it with a calm disposition and a tolerance for mistakes?
- Developing highly effective listening skills with your child is an excellent way to demonstrate that

you're a calm and reasonable person who values their child.

- When discussing situations with your child that may be on the news or perhaps issues that have happened at school, always look to being compassionate in how you interpret the situation. Definitely steer clear of the 'blame game' and from talking inappropriately about anyone. Here you're teaching your child that you respect the integrity of others even though the situation may be difficult.
- When your child talks about their problems or issues, you can open up their thinking to think of others.

'I understand that you were hurt with rough play, but I wonder if others also felt that pain?'

- Sharing and collaborating are great skills to develop. Where possible, teach your child to be inclusive and to reach out to others. Demonstrate this in your own life when dealing with others. For example:

'Those chocolates that grandma gave you look yummy. Do you plan on sharing them with your friends?'

The idea here is to encourage thinking of others as more important in sharing in the pleasure than simply eating them alone.

- When the opportunity presents, invite people into your child's life. This teaches them that there is a joy in sharing experiences.

- Being inclusive with invitations to birthday parties or family social events teaches your child to enjoy the company of many and varied people.

'It's not our job to toughen our children up to face a cruel and heartless world. It's our job to raise children who will make the world a little less cruel and heartless.'
– **LR Knost**

Some children need more attention

Have you noticed how some children demand more attention than others?

I've often wondered about this as we can easily see in classrooms how each child responds differently to their teacher.

There are many myths and stories around why this is so, but I've come to the conclusion that some children need more attention because it's simply part of their personality. It's often the case that if they over demand from parents, they often over demand from others. Think about those adults you know who have a personality type that is more 'out there'. Sometimes they're not great listeners and seem to have too much to say and this can be very off putting to the listener.

Of course, there can be legitimate reasons for a child demanding more attention. If the behaviour is extreme, this needs to be explored with various support groups such as teachers and counsellors. But, firstly, let's see the positive here. A child is keen to be actively engaged and this can be a good thing – in moderation. However, repeated bouts of behaviour that draw attention to themselves can be self-destructive and the child isn't learning the best ways to be effective as a communicator.

It's a slow and steady process which does require trying to set up positive reinforcement for the child when they successfully change their behaviour.

I suggest the following ideas may be helpful in working on changing their behaviours:

- Set up a time when you sit and talk about an issue. Make sure you affirm their voice first. For example:

> *'I'm very impressed that you want to be part of so many conversations. It can be tricky when we all talk at once.'*

- Discuss how taking turns in conversations is a positive thing to do. Discuss a simple plan to affirm your child when they practise slowing down and listening to others. Perhaps agree that if they listen well and wait, you can give them extra time to talk at the end.

- Play games with the whole family that encourages sharing and waiting patiently for each person to have their say and their go.

Some parents have found it useful to promise extra chat time before bed when their children demonstrated they could listen. I know one family who accumulated the time. For every time the child waited patiently, they added an extra few minutes onto night chats.

When working with children, I've found that if you simply sit and listen with intent in an uninterrupted time, they feel quite satisfied. So much of our time in listening is done on the run. Active listening is so helpful for these children as you're gently repeating and reflecting back on what they've said. On so many occasions, children don't really think we're truly listening and just continue with negative attention seeking behaviour.

Don't forget to celebrate when they actually slow down and listen. For example:

> *'Well done. You listened to your brother so well.*
> *I'm wondering what you want to say now?'*

Watch your body language around these children. They're very aware that you're sensitive to their repeated calls for attention. If we appear very irritated, the behaviour can actually escalate. Try and remain calm and gently remind them about how they're great talkers but need to wait and listen.

As a family, practise silence for a few minutes. Many schools use yoga or meditation to train children into enjoying and understanding silence. Some families have a minute silence before they all chat about their day or eat a meal.

Remember, attention seeking can be for many reasons. The above thoughts reflect on helping a child feel reassured that their voice is strong and valued in the family.

Being still and present

Remember the old saying, 'children should be seen and not heard'. It should be more like 'children should be seen and *really* heard.'

How hard is this to achieve when the family home is such a busy place with many competing interests across the week?

In my experience working as a principal, attending to a child when they have something important to talk about, gives you the optimum opportunity to hear the problem and the child feels that they have been really heard.

I would often hear children say, 'My parents don't listen to me.' And they're really saying that they don't have the opportunity to be properly heard or that their feelings are not given value and credibility. Sometimes this can be done easily and other times a family needs to coordinate a set time to have such engagements.

Being present with your child involves giving all your time and attention to them without distractions. It involves maintaining eye contact and listening without interrupting or not showing body language that can be judgemental. It's about being calm, silent and listening with an open heart.

By maintaining this state, children feel that they have the space to keep talking and that it's a safe and respectful space where they can say anything. After your child has spoken, talk about how you were in a privileged position to discuss their thoughts and feelings. This is without bias and without being too quick to judge.

This deep form of listening opens up so many opportunities for a child because they feel valued. Doors close on conversations quickly when interruptions or changed body language occurs. As a parent, it's about that one-on-one time with your child.

I often found that once a child has been really heard, they are more in tune with working out solutions. Keep in mind that children gravitate around family members that calmly and respectfully listen. I believe this applies to all of us!

Chapter 12

Teaching your children

Teaching cooperation

Cooperation comes quite naturally to some of us and others need to be taught. It's best to realise that teaching your child about cooperation is a safe way to ensure that they value it. As children grow, they pass through various stages and self-centredness is one of them and it's not always natural that cooperation will automatically follow.

We need to demonstrate in our own lives that we're cooperative people. In a family setting, there are many occasions when cooperating is required. The trick here is to ensure that your child recognises cooperation as an important tool to use in their life.

Schools work diligently to ensure that children see cooperation as a critical part of their daily work. Teachers will often place children in groups and expect that through cooperation and teamwork children will come to the best outcome. While this is a skill expected and demanded of children at school, it sometimes needs to be reinforced at home. When siblings are struggling to share, or if the eldest child takes control and demands their way, this can be an opportunity to teach cooperation.

Parents should use domestic occasions to ensure that cooperation is part of family life. This can be done through negotiation or when families are doing activities together and a discussion is had about how everyone can work better as a team. Playing formal games together is an excellent way to teach cooperation where using the word 'cooperation' often in conversation is vital. Point out when they use cooperation for a better collective outcome. For example:

> *'Well done! You both cooperated in that game and through your combined efforts you won.'*

If you're watching television or a movie together and there's clear evidence of cooperation in a scene, talk about it.

Obvious areas where cooperation boldly stands out is sport. Without cooperation and teamwork, sport isn't possible. Talk to your children about skilled netball and basketball teams that succeed due to their highly efficient teamwork and cooperative style.

Here are a few thoughts on focussing on cooperation in the family context:

- Let your child see that you use cooperation in your life as a means to be successful; perhaps discuss a work situation where cooperation is used regularly.

- Read books with your child, that have themes of cooperation and team work.

- When supporting your child in school-based activities – such as sports days – talk about how your child used cooperation to be successful or, at an open school day, you can see project work that your child has worked on in a group.
- While driving in the car, you can see cooperation everywhere: talk about the crossing lady and how people cross the road using cooperation to be safe and efficient.
- At the end of a school day, it's worth asking,

'Did you use cooperation to be successful today?'

By teaching your child about cooperation, you're raising their awareness that its part of their world and, by using it, you become a well-rounded person. Further, the more you rely on it, the less self-centred you become in your decision making therefore achieving intellectual growth. It becomes a spontaneous way of life.

'Alone we are smart.
Together we are brilliant.'
– Steven Anderson

Letting the village teach your child

Have we ever thought about where our children actually do their learning? Consider the formal learning that schools provide for students. It's often said that parents are the first educators of their children and this makes sense when you consider the tight bond and relationship that begins from birth.

The amazing influence that the community and extended family have in teaching your child is often understated. I think of how the African proverb 'it takes a village to raise a child' is so needed in our modern society where self-sufficiency and independence are sought. Children need to understand the collaborative nature of their learning and not just look to you, the parent, as the keeper of all knowledge.

External sources play an important role in educating our children; call it education on the run. A child listens and learns in various ways. Some people may impress them more than others and some people are just interesting to be around. Discussions about sport, historical events, local issues and so on are all part of the snippets of information a child acquires in life. Children also learn socially and emotionally from observing how adults interact, what they say to each other and how they operate in public. Children will store this information and interpret it in their own way when they experiment in dealing with other people. For example, how does your family interact with the elderly? If your child is fortunate to have extended family then they learn many valuable lessons from their wise, older family members.

Unfortunately, the village concept has broken down in modern society and children can't roam around idly picking up information as casually as before. Hence, many of our children's contacts are contrived and they have less spontaneous opportunities to learn from different groups of people.

In planning their curriculum, teachers are always looking for opportunities to go on excursions so that children can engage with the real world and learn new ways of being and doing. Parents alone can't provide the rich breadth of learning that comes from broader society and there are sometimes social anxieties about letting other people into their child's life.

However, extreme control denies children their right to learn about difference and interpret for themselves how the world spins. They also need to understand the collaborative nature of their learning, as mentioned in an earlier section of this book.

Here are some practical suggestions to highlight the importance of the village for yourself and your child:

- When you go shopping, invite your child to negotiate with the shopkeeper and discuss products, value for money and so on. Such dialogue is inviting your child to see how different aspects of commerce works.
- Take your child on excursions where they actually engage with people displaying real skills. A trip to the market is a good start.
- Interactions with older adults is important. If not in your own family circle but through other networks. A child can learn so much from older generations.
- A child can learn about different cultures if they're exposed to and interact with people from different cultural and linguistic backgrounds. Check out various cultural festivals and take your child to enjoy the food, music and stories at these festivals. Take your child to culturally specific shopping

centres to smell and taste different foods and hear unfamiliar languages being spoken.

- Think about you neighbours. Are they young or old? Do they have interesting lives to talk to your children about? I often think of some older couples from Italy who generously bake extra pastries to give to the other families in the street. These children have learnt a lot about old traditions and cultural variations by simply having people around them that come from a different set of experiences.

- Encourage your children to engage with all variance of children in their class. Teach them that being exclusive in friendships isn't as adventurous as meeting and learning about other children from different experiences. A school is an excellent environment to learn about the broad nature of the village.

- When your child has a play date at another family home, they're exposed to different family structures, routines and behaviours and this is another way of learning about how families work.

- Being cautious and responsible is necessary, but it shouldn't be so constrictive that a child is only exposed to things that are familiar. Difference is what makes the world so interesting.

- Show your children how you welcome different people and experiences into your life that take you out of your comfort zones. Demonstrate how you learn surprisingly different experiences by being inclusive and not exclusive.

- Draw to your child's attention all the differences of their teachers – they all come from various aspects of life and demonstrate different styles of teaching.
- If you move to a new house, there is a whole new environment to learn about. Explore it with your child.
- Are there interesting family members who have wonderful family stories of the past? Children need to learn lessons from the past to understand their present time.

We need to start thinking about collective dreams, collaborating with others and recognising that we grow and learn through cooperation and teamwork. This recipe of respecting and valuing others' opinions, enjoying the differences between us and constantly looking for and checking into the village in our life is nourishing for the soul.

Chapter 13

The home

Find conversation spaces

The days can be so complex, busy, noisy and emotionally crowded. Everyone wants your time and attention. Finding time to just talk to your child without interruptions can be difficult.

Do days pass when you wonder if you've had any real conversations with your child other than giving instructions or talking about the practicality of the day? You can often feel as though real conversation has passed you by.

I'll now discuss how you can seek out occasions to have conversations without other factors getting in the way. It's about finding emotional space to talk about a topic that might be on the mind of your child or yourself. It doesn't need to have any specific direction, other than a pleasant conversation between the two of you.

Many parents find small conversations in the car work well. Sometimes, the simplicity of sitting in a car together which is uncomplicated and not invaded by other people can be a great time to talk about something on your mind.

Bedtime is often seen as a time to have small conversations together. Some parents tell me that when they're snuggled up watching a movie with their child that this environment can bring out great conversations. Remember these are pleasant together times where conversation is simply enjoyed between the two of you.

Think about the times when you're cooking or playing together; find occasional spaces when real conversation can be had by both of you. It's amazing how powerful statements can be made in the most ordinary of circumstances. Never underestimate how these occasions can be helpful in really talking with your child. These are honest moments and are truly authentic. Most importantly, they're enjoyed by both parties.

When working with children, I would sometimes go for a walk in the schoolyard and talk about the environment with the children. It was surprising how calm and comfortable a child would feel in talking to me. Make your conversation spaces a popular time for your child to talk to you without complication, judgement or interruptions. Walk with them in and through conversation.

> *'Development is a series of rebirths.'*
> **– Maria Montessori**

Creating space between yourself and your child

When your child is very young, it's natural to keep the bond between you strong and you will spend a lot of time attaching to your child. However, as they grow and attend school, you'll eventually spend less time with them throughout the day.

All these changes are natural and expected. A child is gradually developing independence in a variety of ways once their world broadens to kindergarten, school, sporting clubs and so on. It's valuable to find some personal time for yourself in the midst of being a busy parent.

By giving yourself space, you remind yourself that you need to be valued and that personal space can be a form of strengthening your relationship with your child. You come back refreshed and ready to get on with all the responsibilities that you have as a parent.

An important aspect to creating some personal space is to teach your child that even though their development and needs are given the highest priority, you also need to keep nourishing yourself as an adult. If we spend every wakeful hour with our child, we don't give them a chance to breathe in a different space. They need to grow in awareness that their parents are adults and they too need their own form of comfort and support.

A child can become excited and joyful in knowing that you're enjoying yourself, independent of them. This helps them become less selfish and recognise that supporting your personal space is a way of caring for you. The more your child sees themselves as part of a family where all members need support – not just themselves – the more emotional growth steps in and broadens their young horizons.

> *'If you want to be happy, be.'*
> **– Leo Tolstoy**

The importance of rituals in family life

Do you have any family rituals? This could be a range of occasions where you gather together to reinforce or celebrate aspects of family life. You're probably doing this on the run, as it's common practice to repeat patterns within a family.

This is important for several reasons:

- Children learn from routine and feel reassured that what they're doing is part of regular life.

- Rituals are unique to your family. For example, it might be a habit in your house that every Sunday you have a special family meal together. It could be that every Friday night the family has takeaway for dinner and talk about their week. Perhaps your family has a religious ritual on a regular basis.

- Reading at night is an act that becomes very familiar to your child. It reminds them that reading is a way of life in your family.

- Giving your child an awareness that ritual is important makes a clear statement of who you are as a family.

- Consider listing all the rituals and habits that you do and enjoy as a family. Talk about how new rituals can come into play as the family gets older and needs to change, but that there are also rituals that may never change – they're embedded in the family DNA.

- Talk about the difference your children have noticed when they visit other families. This gives them a stronger awareness of what is unique to your family.

- Point out other rituals you notice in organisations.

- School have their own unique cultures. These cultures are made up of routines and rituals that are often unique to any particular school. Children become familiar with how that culture operates and this gives them guidance in how they work and play in that space.

Consider the following:

- Rituals are often passed on from generation to generation.
- Children need and love routine and patterns that they understand.
- Rituals have messages behind them and teach children what is valued and precious in your family. Children naturally compare, and having their own rituals gives them a sense of pride and security in what is recognised as their unique family.
- Sometimes children will reject or work against the family rituals. This is their way of testing their own developing opinions and values. In the long haul, whether they like them or not, they still appreciate the ritual as a statement of what is important to you.

Family is a very powerful part of a child's developing world and family rituals are deeply embedded in the heart and mind of a child for a very long time. When your child becomes a parent, they will reflect on what rituals were passed down to them in their childhood. Surprisingly, many reappear wrapped in the framework of a new generation.

Limits

This can be a tricky one for some families. Where and what constitutes a limit? How do you manage setting limits that are different from other families? Can limits vary from situation to situation?

Let's discuss why limits are important. Boundaries are necessary to give to children, so that they know exactly what they're dealing with and also to give clear and accurate directions to them. If a child has no understanding of boundaries, they can't measure success, achievement and, above all, they have no awareness of what standards you have. In most situations, they do want to please you, and giving no direction only confuses them. Children do expect such guidance from their parents; imagine starting a job without a set of criteria and rules to govern how you work.

Every family should have a strong policy of setting boundaries as part of their family life. The boundaries you set may be different from other families; your expectations and family circumstances are unique to yourselves.

Of course, there will be challenges. In fact, children stretch limits, and this challenge is a good time for families to discuss their values and to adjust boundaries as they see children grow and cope with different challenges. Setting limits is also about managing your parenting.

Remember, setting boundaries gives you the ability to reflect on your own parenting. This might mean changing directions from time to time and being flexible when boundaries need adjusting as your child grows into more demanding situations.

Consider the following thoughts when setting boundaries for children:

- Be clear in what you say and keep the directions simple.

- Set a boundary that is within reason for your child's age. For example:

  *'You can play in the front yard,
  but don't go beyond the gate'*

  *'You can go to that party; however,
  I'll pick you up at 10 pm.'*

- Remember that a boundary should be natural and the consequences logical if a child stretches the limits.
- Ensure that when you set a limit, it's fair and just. It's also important that your child understands why you've set the limit.
- Keep in mind that the limits may change. Regular affirmation of your child is helpful when limits are honoured.
- Discuss as a family why setting limits is important to you as the parent. In the discussion, highlight how it helps you support their needs and at the same time supports your responsible parenting.

Teachers discuss limits intermittently throughout the day. They wouldn't be able to teach effectively without the ability to set limits. It could be regarding curriculum, discipline, setting goals and so on.

Children understand that setting limits gives them direction, strengthens self-discipline and further builds cooperation between teacher and child. They have a better understanding of what is expected of them and they can assess how successful they were in the light of the limits and goals set.

There are no surprises that a child will challenge limits from time to time and that family tension becomes a growth curve for everyone. It's a natural tension that, if handled carefully and with respect of both parties, ensures that child and parent grow together.

> 'Caring for children is a dance between setting appropriate limits as caretakers and avoiding unnecessary power struggles that result in unhappiness.'
> – **Charlotte Sophia Kasl**

How is the environment at home?

Have you ever been in a home that is cluttered or perhaps so tidy that you're scared to move? Have you been in a house where there are many delicate items which can break easily? We all have our own personal way in which we design and enjoy our home space. Research tells us that we all respond differently to space and in the case of our children, this is definitely true.

Is your home designed to allow children to move freely or is it too rigid in the layout? Is your home a source of anxiety for you when children are around? Are there aspects of your house where family gather and also a quiet spot for doing homework?

As mentioned earlier in Part One's nine parenting tips, there are simple changes to the layout of the house that can be made to suit happy family living. Consider the noise levels in the home, especially with the location of televisions. Our anxiety increases if our home isn't set up to comfortably work around a family.

Needs change as children get older. I believe there is value in involving the child in decisions which effect their movement in and around a home. Usually, younger children want to be close to their parents. As they grow, they need their own space and certainly value their own room if possible.

Remember, how we move and operate in the house is teaching our children many values. I always remember a child asking me to visit their home but to remember to take off my shoes at the door as mum would like that. I brought slippers!

Chapter 14

Learning from our children

Our children can teach us so much

Isn't it wonderful how much joy we gain from watching our children? Their laughter, childish ways, imagination and sense of fun gives us life.

Here I invite you to stop and reflect on how children are a source of joy. We can learn so much about the beauty of life through their eyes. After all, being an adult can be very boring. It can also drain our sense of fun and reduce our awareness of everything life-giving around us.

Let your child show you the way to being lighter and more positive about life.

At school, I made it common practice that if I was a having a bad day, weighed down by various things, I would take myself around to the classrooms just to enjoy the chatter, humour and life of the children. It lifted my spirits and made me realise how much I can learn from them. Let's consider our children's youthfulness as a happy pill and one that puts us in a better mental framework.

Their simple wisdom, unshakeable love for their parents and innocence when it comes to seeing the best or worse in a situation teaches us that sometimes we can adopt a lighter and more manageable approach to life. We can begin to understand life from different and less judgemental eyes.

Here are some thoughts that invite us to reflect on times with our children that can be beneficial for improving our spirit and disposition:

- Laugh with your children. See the funny side to their actions.

- Listen to their words. Often, they're simply expressed but with powerful messages.

- Watch them play and join in the experience. They often talk about all sorts of interesting things when playing. It's especially enjoyable listening to their chatter in a sandpit.

- Children love to draw. Watch them and talk about what their drawings are all about. As an adult, doodling can be another form of drawing. This can be relaxing.

- Sing with your child. You'll know some of the songs and the repetition is often comforting.

- Enjoy the changing expressions on their faces and the interesting body language. These shift so regularly and are a key to how they're processing information.

- Let your child know that you learn from them. For example:

    'I love the way you use Play-Doh. Can you show me how you created that shape?'

- Children have a different sense of time than busy adults. Perhaps we can take more time to do things we enjoy and reduce the busy, unimportant things we do that clutter the day.
- Allow children to be creative. This can go in many directions that will surprise you. Their creativity unfolds in so many ways.
- Talk to your children about the fun parts of your childhood; what made you laugh and what drove your spirit.

I invite you to simply enjoy moments with your children and to notice their unique childlike manner. Time passes quickly and those moments where we learn from our children become less and less as they grow older. My belief is that if we capture their joy, we will carry it with us, and it will give us some positive experiences and feelings along the way.

Let your child show you the way to being lighter in life. Adopt a little of their liveliness and enjoy the day.

> *'If you carry your childhood with you, you never become older.'*
> **– Tom Stoppard**

Try being child-like

One of the great advantages of being a parent is that your child will take you through all the stages of growth: physical, intellectual, social and emotional. They will reintroduce you to childlike ways and this can be great therapy!

While I appreciate our children can be exhausting and frustrating from time to time, they do give us such wonderful opportunities to relive our childhood in some way. Perhaps your childhood wasn't so much fun; now is the time to enjoy the innocence and simple joy of being a child with your own child.

Sometimes being an adult and maintaining the pressure of living up to expectations can be very waring, so it's important to share in some fun and uncomplicated joy with your child. It also demonstrates to your child that you can relax and share in their world, with all its magic and imagination. You're valuing their world and not placing expectations on them to be sensible or grown up.

When working with children, I was very blessed to have a school as a workplace. If I wanted to ease the pressure of the office, I would often enjoy playing the games in the schoolyard with the students, join in netball games and share in singing in the choir. I certainly felt better from being part of their world and I would return to the office feeling refreshed.

Consider these points:

- Play in the sandpit with your child. Beaches are wonderful spaces to play in the sand, no matter what age a child is, and they provide a wonderful climate to play all sorts of sports and activities. Notice all the fun families have on beaches in summer. Beaches provide entertainment for all.
- Play formal games at home. Simple boardgames such as Monopoly can provide hours of fun.
- Play Lego with your children. Are you as creative or as skilled as them?

- Drama is a great imaginative tool. Act out simple plays and stories together. Children love the dress ups; join in with them. Sometimes using music and singing together leads to much joy.
- Doing physical activities such as bike riding or rollerblading together in the park can lead to so much enjoyment.
- Children love to write imaginative stories. You can join in and add sections to it.
- Draw together. Using chalk on the concrete is a fun and new way to draw.
- Invite your child to recommend the game and join in. Younger children are very quick to create stories and adventures.

These considerations may not be new to you, but the following reasoning behind these suggestions might be:

- It's good for your mental health to play and relax. What better way than to do it with your children.
- By joining in with your child, you relive some memories and produce smiles. This is positive for everyone concerned.
- Finally, who says we have to lose our sense of being a child and grow up?

A better-balanced adult, who can see life from many angles, is a more interesting and emotionally intelligent person.

> 'Be small and childlike. There is no simpler,
> better way to see the big picture.'
> **– Linus Mundy**

Chapter 15

The bond between parent and child

The importance of keeping attachment strong

Attachment between a parent and child starts well before birth. The desire to attach, be comforted and feel secure is a precious and necessary part of our development. Young parents work hard to ensure that bonding happens early with their infant. As their child grows and reaches out for independence, the need to be strongly attached is still ever-present, but it takes on different forms.

When a child starts school, there are giant leaps in the desire to develop independence but be aware that they still want their attachment with their parents to be strong and consistent. As they reach out for independence, consider the following important suggestions which contribute to healthy bonding:

- From time to time, simply repeat how much you love them – perhaps you love all the precious things they do. This sends a message that that you're bonded to them through unconditional love.

- When they reach for more independence, reassure them that you're always available. For example:

    'It sounds like you really want to walk home by yourself, just remember I'm around if you need me.'

- Talk to your child about what makes them feel happy. Do they trust that you're always present for them even in difficult times? This is worthy of discussion.

- As a family, are you openly affectionate? Being affectionate with cuddles and closely sitting together is an important part of feeling bonded. This can happen with children of all ages. There isn't a time of growing out of this habit, although as a teenager they may give you some grief about being affectionate around their peers. This is natural!

- If you were fortunate enough to have loving parents yourself, talk about how you felt attached to your parents. What special gifts did they have which brought you together?

- Do practical, happy activities together such as singing, dancing and camping. All these ongoing activities remind your child that they're happily attached to you by sharing common grounds when it comes to enjoying life.

Throughout their growing years, keeping attachment steady is all about reassuring your child that whatever the growth curves you encounter, you still love them unconditionally.

To keep your family attachment strong, you need to work on building the family story together and sharing in substantial parts of each other's lives across different periods.

> *'The propensity to makes strong bonds to particular individuals is a basic component of human nature.'*
> **– John Bowlby**

How important is it to always be the winner with your child?

Ever thought about your tolerance level compared to others? Perhaps you've noticed some people who have very high tolerance and seem unaware of behaviour that you would find unacceptable. Sometimes we feel that if we let our children get away with certain issues, that they will be completely lost, out of control and unmanageable.

However, we can still let go and find great success in managing our children. I've often reflected on all the children that went through my schools and I was fortunate to keep in touch with many of them, so I had the joy of watching these children grow to young adulthood. Despite the struggles of parents and ups and downs in the family, most children grew into wonderfully well-rounded adults.

What I learned is that sometimes we take everything so seriously in rearing our children and they know and read our values very well. They also see how we live with them and around others. They notice our moods and temperaments and will often connect with us, as long as we're approachable.

Above all, we need to set the scene to allow our children to engage comfortably with us. Sometimes we outline valid points in our conversations, but most of the time we aim to negotiate so that they also feel like the winner. There are no rewards in parenting for being right all the time and in insisting on having your way. That borders on control and too much use of power.

Consider the following:

- Be patient and understand that each situation isn't the end of the world. It will pass and there will be other occasions to discuss issues as time goes by.
- Put things into proportion, it's a child's problem and should be understood in that context. It will definitely pass and be replaced by yet another situation.
- Consider the long haul. You'll be in discussion and negotiation with your child for years to come, so make it an enjoyable process for both of you.
- Sometimes letting go of principles can be the best outcome. Holding onto old principles can sometimes drag both yourself and your child down. Check in with yourself to see if what you're holding onto is worth the anxiety.
- Take a positive outlook to negotiation with your child and remind yourself how privileged you are to have this opportunity. Happily exchanging thoughts and ideas with them is a precious part of being a parent. Savour the occasions.
- Remind yourself that the child you're talking to now will be changing in the next few years. What does that mean for negotiations? It means that

fairness and understanding should always prevail in conversation no matter what age the child is at the time.

Teachers who have the privilege of teaching children more than once across their primary life will often talk about how a child had grown, responding to different situations. Nothing is static with children. Therefore, how we work, play or negotiate with our children should also be organic; it should shift according to circumstances.

Our children are slowly learning about the human condition. When they engage with us, we need to let them see how justice and reason prevail at any age.

> *'Reduce life to its essence.*
> *It's mostly loving that matters … and last.'*
> **– Linus Mundy**

The art of letting go

Have you ever noticed how your life just gets busier and busier?

In fact, the more complications and busier schedule we have, the more we think we're functioning effectively as a society. Often, I would hear parents at school say that their children were growing up far too quickly and that they were missing out on so much of their childhood, yet they didn't know how to change that situation. There is a lot of truth in this statement, especially given that time moves so fast when we're busy people.

Here I challenge you to find that time by uncluttering life so that space is created for your child. It's not about creating more space, but rather, taking back some time from your already busy life.

This is a massive challenge for families. However, it's possible to declutter life a little to make more room for your children. It wasn't uncommon to hear children at school talk excitedly about plans that their families had made simply to be together.

Consider the following suggestions to reclaim time for the family:

- As a family, plan together special times. This is quite common in some families to gather and plan how each week, fortnight and term has adequate quality time for all of the family. It's a matter of looking at what has to go. It's amazing how creative children can be when included in this discussion.

- Draw up a list of everything that you've scheduled for the week. Can you eliminate some of the activities to just be home with the children? Writing it down works for some families as they see and think about how relevant some of the activities are. Again, involving children in this process is valuable.

- Schools provide occasions of inviting families into the classroom throughout the year and these are great opportunities to spend quality time with your child. Schools understand the importance of building strong families.

- Be creative with your time together. When driving your child somewhere or shopping together, have you got time to stop off for a milkshake or a play in the park?

- Consider the layout of your house. Is it set up so that the children are visible? This enables more conversation, more connection and happy times together.
- Are there activities that you can share together? For example, if you like certain music, invite your child to listen with you.
- Consider picking up your child early from school occasionally to have time together. This can be built in across the year.
- Sitting together and cuddling is quality time, uncomplicated by having to be or do anything.
- Try avoiding saying to your child,

> *'I haven't got time now.'*

Instead say:

> *'That's important. I'll find time to do that with you.'*

> With such a promise, *make sure it's always followed through.*

- Keep a journal of special moments together. Writing it down often stimulates the desire for creating more time together. Show the diary to your child.

- Take care with formalised sports or other extracurricular activities. As parents, we become very involved with them and this consumes time. However, think about kicking a ball around or shooting goals with them at home.

- Set up a schedule on the fridge which highlights time together. This is a clear message to children of their relevance in your life across the week.

- Letting go of jobs is accepting that limits must be set on practical tasks so that you can spend more play time with your child. How often do we miss the laughter and joy of those special moments as they grow from infancy to adolescents? The fatigue or tiredness we often feel is due to the many jobs we put on the to-do list. This fatigue dulls our ability to enjoy our children.

As time goes, the relevance of those busy tasks fades into oblivion but not the journey and the long-term memory of watching your child grow.

> *'In family relationships, love is really spelled t-i-m-e'*
> **– Dieter F Uchtdorf**

Always try to tell the truth

As parents, we all try to protect our children in many ways. They're our responsibility and this includes protecting them emotionally as well as physically, socially and intellectually. At an early age, they're totally dependent on us, which gives our role a stronger dimension. We're always on the lookout to ensure that they're surrounded by love and total care. How wonderful is that? We understand our accountability.

When protecting our children, we should also be preparing them for the real world and with this may come some disappointments and sorrows. It's easy for parents to tell a small lie to protect their child from some impending issue or harm, but this is passively disadvantaging the child who needs and deserves to hear the truth. They rely on your truth to understand the world and to feel secure in it. If they're uncertain that you're not sharing the truth, they might go to other less reputable sources to seek out information. Do they want to do this? The answer is no. They want the truth from you.

By gently disclosing the truth, you're bringing your child into the real world. You're telling them, 'I respect your right to know the truth and I'll give it to you in a way that is suitable for your age and appropriate for your understanding.' Children who are suddenly thrust into critical truths – such as death and divorce –have no choice but to grapple with it and often in a complicated way.

The more we talk to our children in a way that always discloses the truth, the more we will give them the credibility of being able to grow emotionally through many issues.

When working with children, they would often say that their parents hadn't told them about something as they did not want to upset them. You'd be surprised how aware they actually are of watered-down truths. This is dangerous, as children can begin to develop anxiety around all sorts of possibilities.

Here are a few tips in setting the groundwork to talk truthfully about uncomfortable situations or events:

- Lead into a conversation well prepared and choose the time carefully. For example:

    'I would like to talk to you about ... as it's been a difficult problem.'

- Tell the story gently and calmly.
- Give your child time to absorb what you had to say.
- They will ask questions, and this is a time to carefully outline the situation with sensitivity to their age.
- After telling them the situation, check in that they understood what you were telling them.
- Reassure them that the matter is being dealt with and as time goes you will talk to them about related matters.
- Using simple truths is ultimately better. For example:

    'You can't have sweets as it's dinner time soon.'

    This is more realistic than saying:

    'You can't have sweets because your teeth will rot.'

The first statement is real and genuine.

Children deserve the truth. If a responsible parent capably and sensitively presents the truth to their child, they feel secure and reassured. They will return to the correct source, the parent, and ask questions with more confidence and trust.

'If you tell the truth, you don't have to remember anything'
– Mark Twain

Chapter 16

Siblings

It's just sibling business

Do you often wonder if and when to interfere when siblings get angry with each other? Most parents try to settle the affairs with the best of intentions but, sometimes, is it necessary to interfere all at?

Let's remind ourselves that our children are significantly different in temperament, attitude to life and capacity to solve issues. No child develops in exactly the same way.

The order of siblings can also create a difference. Generally, first children are more cautious, second children are more robust and by the time you get to third and/or fourth, they develop considerable survival and resilience skills, as parents have considerable experience and more ease in parenting.

Teachers are always commenting on how different children in the same family learn and how they process information differently. Let's celebrate this difference rather than feel the frustration of managing our children.

When should we step into our children's arguments and when shouldn't we?

When siblings fight, consider the following:

- Is this issue worth my involvement?

- Is the conflict causing considerable distress to one of the children?
- Is there bullying of a younger sibling?
- Are their disagreements frequent or just occasional differences which are quite normal?
- Is it always about the same issue?

Once you establish whether you consider your involvement necessary, take care to:

- Talk to both children at separate times in a calm situation.
- Listen with fairness.
- Suggest that some compromises should be made by both parties once the behaviour has been understood.
- Affirm the children when they calmly negotiate.
- Agree to check in later to see if that angry feeling is still there.

By taking these steps, you're further teaching your children the art of negotiation without coming up with solutions yourself –which often don't work well!

When working with children, I was very conscious to consider their individuality and not to refer to their siblings specifically. Every child needs to have a sense of personal space to discuss their own emotional needs and to feel valued for who they are as individuals.

It's also realistic to realise that families are complex settings with growing children, edging for attention with busy parents listening on the run and busy school weeks with many demands.

Here are a few points to help keep the family setting as calm and steady as possible:

- Check in with your children once a week about issues which have caused them to be angry with each other.
- Take care not to react too quickly when conflicts occur. Take your time and in a calm setting, start the conversation.
- Watch your communication with children ensuring that each child is spoken to fairly.

Above all, see the situation as resolvable and recognise that it will pass. Keep everything in proportion and move on from the situation quickly and your children will move on quickly as well.

When one child demands your attention, how do the others cope?

It's a tricky situation when one child is more demanding than the others and this can often be the case in families with several siblings. This can be for many reasons and especially if a child has Autism Spectrum Disorder (ASD) with difficult behaviour that escalates quickly. This can dominate your family time and compromise your quality experiences with other members of the family.

Parents become frustrated as they deal with this ongoing and difficult issue and they can feel remorseful as they don't have the time or energy to give to their other children. One child's behaviour and demands can override the needs of the others. It's important to reflect on the other children in the family and to understand their emotional responses to issues that impact their childhood.

Often, children develop ways of operating when difficult or demanding behaviour from another sibling occurs regularly. They may escape the scene or attempt to solve the problem for their parents, they may even get caught up with thinking that they're to blame. Whatever the reaction, there is one emotion that many children will go through and that's a feeling of anxiety for their parents who might be struggling with their sibling's behaviour.

You might often hear them say:

> *'Is everything okay?'*

They might feel vulnerable and give a lot more hugs or offer to do more around the house. It's common for children to feel anxiety when they see their parents under pressure. Children also feel a sense of loss for the one-on-one time they could have had with their parents; this is a form of grief and resentment can build. This is a difficult situation for parents who only want the very best for all of their children.

Here are a few thoughts on how to reduce your other children's potential feelings of resentment or anxiety:

- Have an open discussion with the siblings one-on-one at regular intervals.

    Ask them:

    > *'Sometimes mum has a difficult time with your brother, and I wonder how you feel about it?'*

Also note they will be particularly worried about you, so try saying this:

'When you see mummy upset with your brother, are you worried about me?'

'On a scale of one to ten how worried are you?'

'Let's find ways that we can have one-on-one time together.'

- Make time in the week to talk to the other children about how they're feeling when difficult behaviour escalates. When an escalation occurs, ensure that you check in with the other siblings in order to bring down their anxieties and reassure them of your coping skills. In particular, keep an eye on your first child as they can sometimes feel the responsibility of the issue.

- It's quite confusing for the other children to understand their role when such behaviour occurs. Plan to have family meetings and talk about everyone's role in the family. These meetings should be when you feel calm and in control. The other siblings' roles definitely aren't to manage the behaviour and they're not responsible for it.

- If a child has some support – such as a counsellor or psychologist – some parents choose to have a session with the counsellor and the other siblings to help the whole family understand the reasons for their sibling's behaviour.

It's important to be reassuring and reduce anxiety for the other siblings who naturally feel your pain and want to help but can feel helpless. It's all about giving them the reassurance that your relationship with them is intact and that you have the responsibility of supporting all your children no matter what their needs are: it's not their responsibility to manage their difficult sibling.

As all of the siblings grow up, in time they will understand the situation better, but the grief of the compromised relationship they had with their parents can still linger and this needs to be understood by the parents.

The difference each child makes

Do you remember your childhood with your own siblings? Now think about how your parents managed the differences and the rivalry, if it happened. Did your childhood relationship with your siblings' impact on your relationship with them now as adults?

This can be a tricky issue for parents and a lot can depend on different factors. These factors could be the age difference between children, the personalities of each child and the feelings of security that each child has of themselves and their relationship with their parents.

I have a long-held belief that in the primary years all children want and need personal time with their parents. Every child craves to be an only child for a while, where they're the centre of attention.

However, at an early age, children have the opportunity to learn about cooperation, patience and collaboration. They grow up in an environment of many voices which is their norm. They often learn on the run and this involves all the ins and outs of growing up with siblings who are also going through their own childhood.

Parents play a key role in establishing a family setting that breeds positive interactions between all members of the family.

The following pointers might be helpful:

- Remember that all children, no matter what age, are entitled to having a voice in the family.
- Mealtime with everyone is an excellent opportunity to share experiences and actually learn to listen to each other.
- If one child feels under the weather with their siblings, find some personal time with them. Take them out of school for an afternoon and chat with them focusing on their needs.
- Remember that they're all individual and some will have skills and talents that are more vocal and obvious than others. Take care to highlight each child's talents and not just the child that is the loudest.
- Play games together as a family. Great skills are learned from playing together. This can include doing group activities together such as camping, cooking and so on.

When children disagree with each other, ensure that you don't become involved but that you do have rules with regard to how disputes between the children should be managed. If a child asks you to intervene, clear guidelines need to be established so that your involvement is understood as a mentor.

One family I knew developed a tradition that on each child's birthday they would have a special treat just with the birthday child and the parents. This worked well for them and everyone in the family understood the purpose. Perhaps developing your own family tradition of how you celebrate each child could be developed. Deciding how to celebrate each other by respecting and valuing each other's individuality would be a wonderful project for the whole family.

We're all so different and in many ways. We can sometimes look at the order of our children to gain insight into understanding their personality. We can detect certain patterns that are common to first children who are generally more conservative whereas the second child usually more robust and a risk taker. It's not uncommon to hear parents comment on how different their children are and yet the upbringing is the same for all of them. The reason is simple: each child is different, and their growth will be unique. Parenting should reflect that each child will have different needs that should be addressed.

In order for each child to be themselves, they will need their own time and space to just simply be themselves. This can be a challenge for parents who sometimes struggle to understand how each child responds differently to the family structure, especially rules and regulations. Rather than being frustrated about this, turn it into a positive. Aren't we lucky to have such variation in our children?

Each child has needs that challenge us to work with them differently. It also challenges us in how we parent. Some children are quiet and more reserved whereas some children are very vocal and demanding. The variations go on indefinitely.

Keep these factors in mind:

- Every child is unique and sometimes this might mean how you work with each child will be different.
- Understand that while you give equal time to your children, it's natural that some children may demand more.
- Recognise that listening to your children will be different for each child.
- You'll need to cater for individual differences and see them as a gift in each child.
- Take care that quieter, less open children will need to be drawn out more into conversation, but you still respect their quiet nature.
- Sometimes as a family, you need to do collective activities. However, it's important to check in with each child as to how they're engaging with family matters.
- You need to be careful in using language that doesn't indicate competition between children.
- Each child will have their own set of strengths that need to be celebrated. There is no need to have all of your children achieving and being successful in the same way. From time to time, some children will shine more than others, and this is normal in an energised family.
- We look for tendencies in our children that remind us of ourselves. Take care that we don't highlight aspects of a child that aren't seen favourably by everyone.

- Take care not to label a child with a particular characteristic. As they grow, especially into teenagers, their personality will keep evolving overtime and with this may come significant changes.

- Given that each child is an individual, be open to surprises with them and relish the little changes that can appear.

When working with children, I was amazed by how insightful children were regarding their parent's perception of them. I soon realised that their sensitivity to their parent's perception of them impacted on how they operated around their parents.

We need to have an open mind and heart to the beauty of the individual child. We need to see their individual changes – no matter how varied and uniquely different from their peers and siblings – as another step in becoming a well-rounded young independent adult.

Chapter 17

Positivity

Celebrating the positive actions of others

Teachers are very conscious to ensure that they model and teach children the value of affirming others when they succeed. For some children, this isn't a difficult awareness to develop but for other children it can take some time as they put their own interests ahead of others. Sport is a typical example of how some children feel frustrated if they don't win and subsequently struggle to enjoy success for other children.

While to some degree children will learn the value of affirming others, there is still the importance of teaching them the value of being happy for other children when they succeed over themselves. By teaching them to be happy for other children, you're giving them wonderful tools to notice and genuinely value others which is a mature way to appreciate people.

In schools, there are various programs designed not only to focus on building resilience when things go wrong, but to also recognise in themselves how mature they are to value the success of others. In saying this, I appreciate that we're dealing with children and their slowly evolving emotions, but the home environment can be a profound learning space for respecting and valuing others.

Here are some suggestions for the home:

- When together as a family, discuss the success of some people you admire. Talk about the difference they make through their skills or gifts.
- Read stories of people you admire to your children.
- Actively acknowledge other children at sport venues or other extracurricular activities that do well.

When your child praises the success of another, tell them how proud you are that they can recognise the successes of another child. For example:

> *'How clever you are to notice John's running skills. Tell me more.'*

Invite the family to write a genuine comment about each other – this can be a positive statement about a strength you notice in that person – and talk about these comments together.

When working with children, especially those who felt badly about their efforts, it was common practice to remind them of the children who spoke highly of them. You give them open sentence starters to talk positively about other children. Often you would start sentences with:

> *'I like Mary because ...'*

> *'John is friendly and ...'*

> *'Joshua has wonderful ...'*

Teachers would often use this tactic in a classroom, inviting all children to write one happy comment about each other. It was amazing how it awakened an appreciation of others and lowered anxiety in the room. It also gave children a strong message about finding the richness in others.

It also touches on learning about your own limits. Think about the people who we like to gravitate towards. There are no surprises that it's people who admire the positive in you.

'I've learned that people will forget what you said, people will forget what you did, but people will never forget how you made them feel.'
– Maya Angelou

Every day is different, even for children

What's in a bad day? Every child will have a bad day. This means that there will be some days where a child just simply isn't as happy or as active or interested as normal. There is a tendency to think that having a bad day is a privilege of adults. Not so!

Sometimes children just aren't feeling their best. This can be for a range of reasons, not dissimilar from an adult. Sometimes tiredness, emotional upsets and disappointments can reduce feelings of contentment temporarily. We're often not fully aware of these feelings, but we know that we're not operating at our best.

What do we do? Just accept that a child has the right to a bad day and lower your expectations and questions. Probing a child as to why they're feeling down can only cause them confusion because they might feel that they must be always operating the same way to make a parent happy.

Remember that a child is keen to be valued by their parents and so they try very hard not to disappoint.

The following are positive phrases for when a child has a bad day:

> *'I sometimes feel down and need time to pick myself up too.'*

> *'Having a low day can give us time to look forward to a better day.'*

> *'Low days are preparing for the better days.'*

> *'When I've a low day, I like to ... have a bath, go for a walk ...'*

The key message is that occasionally having a bad day is normal and you understand, as a parent, that they need some space.

The art of being happy

I've recently read an excellent book, *Positive Psychology Coaching: Putting the science of happiness to work for your clients* (2007) by Ben Dean and Robert Biswas-Diener. While its primary concern is coaching, the book also talks about the value of being happy and how this leads to the development of well-rounded individuals who can form healthy relationships with other people and who demonstrate emotional and social maturity. It's all about thinking healthily.

I then thought about family well-being and the ability of families to generally be happy. There's much to be grateful for in our family life. Consider the simple realities that we sometimes take for granted:

- I actually have a family.
- There is love in my family.
- My daughter smiles at me and says she loves me.
- My son is so funny.
- We all get together on Saturday night and watch a movie.
- My three-year-old just gave me a flower from the garden.

These are simple examples of how we should be happy for all the joys – simple and complex – that we have in our families.

It's certainly easy to feel the negative weighing us down. However, many of the troublesome issues in a family will pass and what will remain are the memories of how we enjoyed the moment. Sometimes, when a family goes through extreme trauma, they come to realise the preciousness of what they've had in their life and this gives them a greater sensitivity to the joys of life.

When working with anxious children, I have very positive memories of including happy sentiments and thoughts into the conversation and it was amazing how the overall tone of the conversation would change when the focus was on happy thoughts. It eases tension and releases pleasant feelings into our body.

We're also teaching our children that we value being happy as a human condition that enables us to live well both mentally and physically. Happiness is contagious; people gravitate around the warmth of positive, happy people. If you can see the happy moment and find laughter as a cure for solving problems, your child will recognise this.

> *'For every minute you are angry, you lose sixty seconds of happiness.'*
> **– Ralph Waldo Emerson**

A house of happy thoughts

Have some fun with your children and at the same time reinforce positive thoughts that you're having about your child.

Children thrive on reassurance and, combined with the element of surprise, they feel quite excited and will always anticipate what's next. It becomes a very pleasant game of reassurance. In a child's bedroom, for example, write little affirming messages and scatter them in different places – under the pillow could be a message:

> *'You have such a great smile.'*

Perhaps in their cup the words:

> *'Thanks for helping me today.'*

The messages can be put in a variety of spaces around the house and of course can change to suit the occasion. A surprise note in the school lunch box or school bag is a wonderful warm and reassuring feeling for a child during the school day. A positively written statement about your child builds their sense of self-worth and reminds them that they're valued. Some children may keep the notes and paste them in a book which is handy to read from time to time. Children will often write loving notes to parents and this is our way of doing the same.

I often bring a child into my office and together we guess where I've left my note; no surprises that they find it very fast!

Checking in on the happiness level of your family

When the family gathers, is there an air of happiness? Families that seem happy and enjoy each other's company tend to talk more together, are noisier and, from my observation, seem to have a well-developed ability and interest in listening to each other. They seem more tolerant of each other's vulnerable sides and will often find humour in the various habits and patterns that members of the family adopt.

We should never underestimate that happiness is actually a strength and that seeing the world in a positive light can set the scene for a family to work.

When emotions like anger, frustration and disappointment dominate a parent's disposition, there's no wonder that a child will close down their communication and develop coping skills around that parent. Such negative emotions displayed by parents, can also be seen by children as a use of power against them. Children very easily sense what buttons will trigger negative emotions in their parents. They will develop their own way of having their needs met, and this sometimes involves going around the parent.

Developing a positive, optimistic mode of operating around each other is most inviting to a child and it's quite contagious. Everyone likes being around a happy and positive person. Of course, life presents challenges and when a parent feels less likely to be optimistic, happy to engage and positive, it's best to let your child know. For example:

*'Today I'm not feeling my best.
I have some things on my mind, but tomorrow will be a better day.'*

This is about alerting your child when to best approach you for advice. It also reduces confusion for children who might usually know you as a happy and positive person.

Keeping a high level of happiness should be a focus for parents. Laugh together and enjoy hearing the delights of each other's experiences. Go into conversation with a positive approach. Find warmth and humour in what they have to tell you. Use affirming language and avoid negative language.

If children hear positive inflection in their parent's conversation, they will respond positively themselves and then be less cautious in talking to their parents, thus feeling emotionally safer.

When working with children, they would sometimes tell me that they would choose not to talk about certain topics to their parents as it made their parents angry. They would be selective in what and how they expressed themselves.

Try some of the following to lighten the load and brighten the day:

- Smile often when talking.
- Have a warm tone in your conversation.
- Use a gentle and calm voice at all times. Sometimes, when they talk about their day, have a laugh and join in the story.
- Applaud their strengths with confidence and warm sentiments.

Some parents have affectionate titles for their children which makes their child feel good. For example:

> 'Thanks, speedy. I always get it on time.'

> 'Hey, handsome, pass me the spoon.'

Tell jokes to each other; children love jokes. I know of one family who have a book of jokes that they read together each week.

> 'Today I feel ten out of ten in being just happy. What's your number?'

This particular message to your child is that taking on a positive and happy disposition enlivens the space in which you live. You're telling them, 'When I feel happy, the world is a better place. Come and join me!'

'Let there be more joy and laughter in your living.'
– Eileen Caddy

Negative thoughts can get us down

Have you ever felt overcome by negative feelings about a range of issues? In this case, I'm referring to your child. Often, it's poor behaviour that you see and want to disassociate with as quickly as possible. In fact, when we see such behaviour, we can have all sorts of related feelings such as:

- You love your child, but you dislike the behaviour. Keep it separate in your thoughts.
- 'I'm a poor parent.'
- 'I don't discipline enough. I should be harder.'
- 'I really try but they don't listen.'
- 'Why are they so nasty?'
- 'I don't like their personality.'

So many feelings come up to the surface and can easily cause us to lose sight of what we're actually dealing with and that is simply a child.

I've heard parents say to me when things seemed gloomy that they felt like dissociating with their child and, of course, they felt guilty because of these feelings. Oh, what an unsettled web we weave in our head when a series of bad behaviour seems to be all-consuming. You can become highly sensitive and on guard as to what the next challenge to your emotional stability may be.

Remind yourself that too many negative thoughts just continue to feed off each other and the problem has, by nature of your anxiety, increased exponentially. Teachers invite children to write positive thoughts about each other in class on a regular basis. This certainly helps reduce anxious personal cobwebs.

To help you put things into perspective, reflect on the following thoughts that come from many years of seeing children grow through their problems developing into well-rounded young adults:

- Keep in mind that the behaviour will pass. It's only a moment in time in the life of your child.
- Your child is just a child, and this is a testing time to express themselves.
- Realise that you won't like some of their behaviour and that's okay.
- Give yourself some space. When you feel overwhelmed, just take a walk.
- Remember that the poor behaviour is normal as children grow.
- Don't compare your child's behaviour to others. This only builds resentment and further negative feelings.
- When your feelings are overwhelming and negative, remind yourself how much you love your child. Think about happy times together. Could you live without them?
- When you have a negative thought about your child, look at some photos of them which reminds you of the beauty and sweetness of your child.

- When you have negative feelings, work harder to have happy times with your child. Keep up the cuddles, laughter and family activities.

- Shorten activities such as homework and have some fun together. Short, sharp bursts of fun together are very healing.

- Talk to your child's teacher about the wonderful things they've noticed about your child. This can often be an eye-opener for parents.

Negative thoughts only inhibit your ability to move on and work through issues calmly and reasonably. The more we fill our head with negative feelings with regard to our children, the further we distance ourselves from developing a rich relationship. Every child deserves that relationship – with or without bad behaviour attached.

> 'We are imperfect humans growing imperfect humans in a world and that's perfectly okay.'
> **– R.L Knost**

Chapter 18

Differences

We all have different ways of seeing the world

Every home is different; every family operates at their own pace and in their own style. This is sometimes complicated by two parents who operate differently around their child when it comes to discipline, generosity and other important issues.

It's hard to teach your children values when other families operate differently. It's not uncommon to hear parents say that the pressure is on them when they don't approve of certain things that happen in other homes. For example, when is the right time to give a child an iPad or phone? What can they watch on television? How much free time do they have? Every family will have their own standards which brings out the best and sometimes worst of their children.

The best advice to give families is to include the following values when setting up arrangements in the family home:

- Firstly, be consistent. If you have a rule, then doing your best in being consistent with that rule will show your child that the rule has value in your eyes.

- Listen with interest when they tell you how other children have more opportunities than themselves. Gently explain that you work under a different plan and that negotiation can be part of it as time moves on. For example, you may have rules about bedtime, however, as your child gets older, that rule can shift to suit their age.
- Technology is a big challenge and setting the rules around its use should be done so that your child is really clear on how it works in your home.
- Have family conferences to look at the rules and conditions that have been set up. They may need some tweaking, and this is a chance to listen to your child about their desire for change.
- Sometimes putting reminders on the fridge is a great way to freshen family values.
- Affirm your child for being part of the family arrangements which can change by negotiation.

I've heard of some families going out to celebrate a successful month of working on home matters. Teaching your child to be inclusive is all about being part of a team.

Whatever the plan is in your home, keep in mind that your child should feel included, understood and valued. What you teach them by doing this is that their opinion matters as a family member.

Teaching children about discrimination

How do we tackle this immense topic with a child? Quite simply, we should be starting at an early age as there are so many examples of discrimination in a child's life. Some are subtle and some are more blatant.

A great sadness for me as school principal was to see how prejudice and discrimination could so easily creep into a child's life. It's ever-present through media, television, poor modelling from families and extended networks. It was often subtle, but children learnt quickly to align themselves to groups and cultures that felt comfortable, seemed similar and made them feel welcome. Such alignment sometimes led to reduced understanding and tolerance of difference as it quickly shut down interest in other viewpoints.

Now, having said that, I can assure families that the best way to strengthen children's understandings of their complex world is to expose them to as much as possible.

If your child has little understanding of disability, perhaps watch the Paralympic Games or talk to neighbours or friends who have a disability. Again, we remind our children that aligning with difference makes us richer.

Starting at an early age is the key. You may have a favourite charity in which the family contributes, talk about why this charity is so important to you. Schools frequently take on projects to raise the awareness of social differences. If your family keeps up the dialogue at home and capitalises on opportunities to engage with social difference, they're encouraging their child to develop a broad appreciation of life.

Of course, everything we say and do as parents can potentially demonstrate bias. It's unavoidable at times. However, we can take care to watch how we talk about groups that are different. If your child hears that you're open to differences and respect the variance in society, they're more receptive to becoming unbiased themselves. They're also more inclined to talk to you about such ideas and issues.

Here are a few tips in this important area:

- Talk positively about differences in our society.
- Always tell your child sentiments such as this: 'While I feel this way towards an issue, there are other perspectives that could be considered.'
- Watch television shows or movies together that cover important areas of discrimination.
- In a child's friendship group there will be children of various races, attitudes, different family backgrounds, social and economic class and so on. Embrace the differences that your child brings home. Learn from the acceptance your child shows towards matters of discrimination.
- Be an opportunist. When you see a chance to engage with someone or something different, include your child.
- Demonstrate to your child that discriminating in any form limits a person's capacity to understand the bigger world. For example,

> *'I'll have my opinion on certain issues or ideas, but I welcome the opportunity to listen to others.'*

Here you teach your child to open their thinking beyond themselves.

It's important to keep the pilot light on for your child to explore, respect and value differences in our world. Our objective as parents is to ignite a desire in our children to learn about everything that is different to what they know. Hopefully they come to it with compassion and understanding.

> *'No one is born hating another person, be of their colour of his skin or his background or his religion. People must learn to hate and if they can learn to hate, they can be taught to love for love comes more naturally to the human heart than its opposite.'*
> **– Nelson Mandela**

Parents are different and that's okay

Who remembers their upbringing? One thing for certain as soon as you become a parent, you begin to reflect on your own upbringing. As your child becomes more independent, patterns of how your parents dealt with various situations will loom large in your mind. It wasn't uncommon for parents to tell me how they found themselves repeating words that their parents had said to them when growing up. Some parents were anxious not to repeat the same child rearing as their parents and so they sometimes overcompensated with their children, which led to other problems.

As parents from different upbringings, we bring to the table different ideas about how to raise our children. There are no surprises that this can cause some tension between parents.

As mentioned through this book, children will also gravitate towards the parent who is less punitive, less judgemental and often more relaxed in their listening. This can sometimes cause more frustration on the part of the other parent who feels that their child needs more discipline.

Here I'll remind you to firstly accept that parents have different understandings of child rearing and together parents bring a lot to the table. There is no absolute right or wrong. The best way to manage this situation is to agree as parents that you're honest with your child in acknowledging that sometimes you'll see things differently. Your child is very aware of this and the more it's understood in the family, the better for everyone. I would also suggest that, as parents, consider attending a small parenting course together. This brings out the differences but especially focuses on how common factors in parenting should be shared.

As a family, discuss important issues together as this will give both parents a chance to look at the issues at hand. Sometimes one parent is better at dealing with one issue and, as a couple, agree on when this should happen. Having a united front can sometimes be overwhelming for your child as they feel they have no place to go in discussing and negotiating their problems.

Both parents could practise the following:

- Never overreact when listening to a situation. After all, you want your child to keep talking. Listen with interest before you ask questions and work through an issue. If you feel that you might overreact to what's being discussed, then I would recommend that this could be a matter for the other parent.

- As parents, being consistent can be difficult at times. This is why discussing all the ins and outs of the situation are important before making decisions.

The more parents make themselves available to their child, the greater the chance of the child being open to both parents in their discussions.

When talking to parents, I noticed that those children who had authentic relationships with their parents felt that home was a safe place to talk. They would often tell me how their parents reacted differently to situations but would comfortably say, 'I can talk to both of my parents.'

It's also helpful to talk to your child about your childhood so that they can understand your own journey. This helps them reflect on the differences in their family.

The one factor parents have in common is that they care for their child and want them to grow up happy and well adjusted. Parents can be different, be capable listeners and genuine in how they communicate with their child.

PART 3

Helping Your Child with School

Chapter 19

The beginning

Pre-school experiences

How many parents worry themselves about whether to put their children into childcare or continue homecare before school? On many occasions, I was asked by young parents if putting their child into a childcare before they go to school disadvantages them. Parents also wonder whether staying home with their child before school gives them more nurture and sets them up to cope better with school. And so, parents question their decisions in their child's early years.

What I can tell you from my experience is that whatever mix the preschool child has, it's more about providing them with balance and quality of care, be it at home or in childcare. There are clearly more opportunities with language and social development in childcare and kindergarten. Children are exposed to various families and are hearing and using language all the time, thus, they quickly adapt and use language with ease.

However, those children who remain at home with a parent, appear calm and steady and have learned a great deal from simply being with their most important role model. On the other hand, kindergarten gives a child many social experiences and they learn how to engage with a variety of people. From my observations, after a few months settling into school, children who have had more time at home and those who have spent their early years at childcare appear to show very little difference in their response to school.

We sometimes underestimate how adaptable our young children can be when given challenges. In the first few months in the first year of school, teachers work on setting up routines and patterns in the classroom which the children are keen to follow. They are busy, full days and the differences between children's preschool experiences fade as the months continue. The first year of school is also a time for children to find themselves socially and begin their focused intellectual journey with formal reading and writing.

Of course, helping your child before starting school by reading stories and learning how to count is also supported at early childcare centres and kindergartens; and all early learning is gratefully appreciated and valued by the school. A child's formal learning, which begins at school, puts them under a different pressure and whether your child has had more years at home doesn't make a great deal of difference once the child is settled at school. It may mean a great deal to you in being the supportive parent and that's a different matter.

This is born out of my own observations and experience of many years observing children as they start school. What's important is that pre-schoolers have a balanced life with stimulus coming from parent input and other influences.

They need plenty of rest, tempered with challenges that engage them in a variety of ways. They need an environment where they can question, feel safe and challenge themselves. A combination of many experiences is the key to setting up your child for a successful start to school.

> *'A child's life is like a piece of paper on which every person leaves a mark.'*
> **– Chinese proverb**

Parents as early educators

You've already taught your child many experiences and they've learnt from your own life journey over the past few years. You've taught them to walk and speak and now they're ready to take on the new adventure of formal learning.

I stress 'formal', as to date, so much learning has been in operation in and around your child. Never underestimate the amount of learning that has already been acquired. This has happened through your modelling, through incidental experiences and exposure to the real world.

The journey now widens, and children will experience exposure to new thinking and new values in a classroom of children and through the school system. As parents, you're significant partners in the education of your child because you're the primary educators. The school compliments your valuable work.

Together with the school, you journey with your child through the next seven primary years of their education.

During this time there will be many adventures, joys, mishaps and powerful learning experiences.

It's important to trust your educators and to feel connected to them when it's important to discuss any matters. Teachers appreciate that they are only part of a child's education.

Parental influence is strong in shaping the work a school does. Relationship with your teacher and school is a key factor in ensuring a happy, well-adjusted child in the school setting.

Being supportive when starting school

There is so much to say about starting school for the very first time. Where to begin?

The earliest experiences are crucial for a positive start. Think about your own images of starting school and I'm certain that how people operated around you was an important factor in feeling good about yourself. Children will look for reinforcement from parents that school is a good place to be. Talk to your child about your own happy experiences. Tell them how proud they make you now that they are going to school. Ensure that the early transition experiences are happy occasions.

Celebrate as a family when your child comes home from school and listen to what they tell you about their day. Boldly display their artwork done at school around the house and make certain that they see you in a happy and relaxed relationship with your teacher. This reassures them that school is an extension of home and a happy place in which you feel satisfied.

This is all about building early trust between home and school.

Try not to talk about the long haul of school life. Young children are only concerned about the present. I always remember a little prep boy appeared at my office in early March, school bag on his back, crying quietly and saying to me, 'Thank you, Mrs Smith, I can go home now because I can read.'

I didn't have the heart to tell him that this was the beginning of a long journey at school over many years! I'm pleased to report that we worked through the problem and he is now a young man who is a qualified engineer.

Prep teacher – a child's perspective

Do you remember your prep teacher? To a child in prep, the teacher is a powerful image in their mind. Parents often bemoan the fact that the prep teacher seems to be first in their child's mind before them!

What this means is that the teacher will have a most impressive impact on your child's life for that first year. This is why children need to hear and see that their family equally values the presence of that teacher in their life. In order for your child to feel secure in that first year, they need reassurance from you that you're in a strong and trusting relationship with their teacher.

If at any point you feel discussion is necessary with the teacher, ensure that your child still feels reassured that everyone is on the same page. When children feel less secure, they will often shut down and not talk as much about their school day.

The good news is that prep teachers are chosen for the very specialised ways they handle children's emotions. Prep teachers are wonderful nurturers and passionate early educators, and skilled in working closely with young families. They also understand that parents are anxious and need to feel a strong connection to their child's first year. Therefore, schools will offer many occasions for parents to join them in the classroom. Try to be present on these occasions as they're precious and memorable for the family.

Finding friends when you first start school

Here I'll discuss feeling connected.

Parents often worry that their child won't bond with other children and might begin to feel isolated.

The good news is that teachers are really switched on when it comes to this issue. Schools usually have a special playground or designated areas whereby prep teachers are rostered on during the breaks. Most schools set up a buddy system where your child has a senior child overseeing them in the yard. This is quite comforting to your child and you, as a parent, will value this support.

All schools are very aware that early days in prep means extra special attention is given to the children settling into school. Within a few weeks, friendships begin to form, and children find small networks of other children to play with. Finding and establishing friends will vary from child to child. Some children just need more time to build themselves a friendship group – and this is quite natural.

Ask your teacher the following questions:

- 'Is my child bonding well with other children?'
- 'Are they on their own during the breaks?'
- 'Do they engage well with other children?'

An occasional check in with the teacher will give you that reassurance.

The thought of our children not making friends at school is heartbreaking. However, we need to give our children space to settle with other children.

Ten easy ways to help children cope with early stress at school

There are many minor anxieties that can easily interfere with happy moments when your child starts school. Children need to feel secure and have success in simple, memorable ways. Early positive feelings have an impact on later success as they fuel more success and happy feelings.

1. Starting school is all about new faces, images, smells, sounds and feelings.

- I suggest:

    Hold your child's hand firmly and stay with them until they're secure in their classroom. Also reassure them that you'll return exactly when school finishes and clearly identify where that will be. This is a promise you must keep.

2. Starting school is all about what others think of you.
   - I suggest:

   Reassure your child that meeting new friends is good. Tell them that you're pleased that they're meeting new children. You're not looking for one particular friend to be established; you welcome all their friends.

3. Understanding the routine of the day can be overwhelming.
   - I suggest:

   Talk to your child about what a routine is and tell them that you'll be happy to hear about all the differences that the day presents.

4. Not all children can talk about their day and, just as we struggle to record our day, they sometimes need time before they disclose the experience of school.
   - I suggest:

   Make a simple chart which starts with one and ends with ten. Then ask them to tell you how the day has gone – is it one out of ten or higher? Sometimes it's easier for children to explain a feeling by using a number rather than talk about a particular situation.

5. A big part of school is feeling success in the schoolyard and, although teachers direct children's movements, it's still within a child's capacity to form their own friendships.
   - I suggest:

   Be careful not to set early high expectations here. Some children who are more verbal will engage quicker with children in the schoolyard. It's important that children feel they can engage with different students and move onto others. Children listening and moving around to different groups suggests their ability to be comfortable in listening and engaging with different students. Encourage your child to learn about many different children. No one personality is the best choice, although this can be difficult as students often want a close friend early in their years at school.

6. Early in term one, children notice differences between themselves. Some children talk more in class and demand more attention while others can move quickly through teacher's expectations and appear to be in control. Other students are quiet and take time to reflect and process what's going on around them.

- I suggest:

Encourage your child to enjoy the experience of just being at school. Explain that enjoying the experience of learning is more important than being the best at any one activity.

7. First term can seem long and tiring after the initial joy of starting has worn off the family. Routine starts to appear and a realisation that being at home with the family may have more to offer.

- I suggest:

From an early stage, remind your child that you're happy that they're attending school and each day makes you feel that they're successful. Sometimes drawing up a chart with each day listed and colouring it in as a success chart really helps them cope with the ordinary side of the day in the first term. It's all about feeling that being at school makes you happy and it's a successful experience. Each day can bring a surprise and a little success.

8. Opinions of others, which include immediate family, are always important to children. Take care to ensure that ancillary discussions around your child are positive in nature. Children pick up conversations quickly which can be destabilising to a good start.

9. School can be a long day. This environment is set up with routines and schedules that are quite different from preschool settings.

- I suggest:

    Give your child plenty of rest and take care not to introduce them too early to extra curricula activities. Teachers have considerable structure to their day which can be tiring for a young student.

10. Children proudly will bring home many samples of work they have completed.

- I suggest:

    Those samples of work are clearly displayed in the home where other members of the family can applaud their efforts and discuss the work. Visual samples of work talk more to a family than some reassuring words.

Starting school isn't about our success as adults and it's not about us feeling that we've performed well. For the child, happy long-term memories of early success at school are all about small steps of progressive achievements fuelled by parent's approval.

Chapter 20

Supporting your child at school

Children and school fatigue

There is a lot of excitement when a child starts school. As the school journey continues, there are many new experiences; exposure to new situations, new friends to meet, learning challenges and so the list continues to grow.

School is an amazingly busy, noisy space in which a child has expectations set for them. It's filled with successes and failures, establishment of friendships and social failures. Also throw into this mix changes in family situations and emotional challenges. For a child, the journey of school is a powerfully embedded, influential part of their overall development. After reading the above, which is by no means an exhaustive list, you might feel a little overwhelmed – and why not?

A child feels and knows that school is all about expectations. Expectations can put strain on a child's emotional capacity and readiness to cope, even if we shroud them in warmth and affirmation.

Thus, children feel and need respite from the emotional exercise of daily attendance at school. Certainly, school holidays give children and family a rest from the rigour of school and routine, but the fatigue I refer to can happen at any time across a child's school journey. If, for example, they've had a series of bad experiences, home situations change or they're generally not feeling well, this can be a trigger to consider a short respite from school.

My belief and experience as a school principal is to respect a child's readiness for a break and to make some changes, if necessary. The world won't come crashing down and the school is always there and available to be supportive.

This principle is the same for an adult. When the kitchen gets too hot, step outside. There is no deafening research to suggest that pushing through stress is the answer. This doesn't make us stronger. What's to be admired and valued is the ability to recognise how to break from the intensity of a situation. If we teach our children strategies to meet the situation head on, we're giving them life skills that ultimately strengthen their resolve and skill in managing stress. The mere fact that they're breaking the routine of school is irrelevant.

So, what does this all mean for our children?

In my many years of experience as a principal, the following thoughts might help if your child is experiencing early school fatigue:

- Recognise that it's legitimate. School fatigue can happen from time to time: it's real and needs to be addressed effectively.
- Talk to your child about the feelings they have and what makes them feel so unsettled.
- Recognising their concern is key to a quick recovery. It also tells your child that you agree they're entitled

to feel overwhelmed and there are ways to abate the problem. The fact that you're listening to their feelings eases their anxiety.

- Brainstorm strategies together to ease their concerns. Sometimes having a small break from school is an excellent strategy. This was one that I would often recommend, much to the surprise of parents.

After the discussion, start to put things in motion. Keep the school well informed and include the teacher in the plan. Often, it's as simple as a short break from the mental routine of school. It's amazing how short breaks can make such a difference to your spirit. Sometimes merely taking your child out of school for a few hours and doing different things together is a refreshing break for all of you.

Schools are predictable spaces with routine and familiarity. How about enjoying the refreshing experience of being in spaces that aren't part of the regular routine?

The key point here is that we acknowledge that school fatigue is real and children – especially those that thrive on creativity in their life – can regularly be stifled by the school environment. A simple break can make such a difference, which ultimately boosts the learning experience.

Keep in mind that children learn when they're happy and feel secure. Having a presence at school isn't always a formula for ongoing improvement and learning.

Friendships are important

As adults, we've developed social skills that ensure that we can form friends. We're socially mature enough to cope with disappointments and to not feel undervalued when friendships end. This is not so with our children, especially in the primary years. This is a time when they're slowly developing their social literacies and developing friendships that they see as a mark of emotional success.

Of course, by nature of their development, the friendships will come and go; some will be sustainable, and others will have bitter, sharp endings which can cause children hurt and confusion.

This is about building social stamina. It also involves building resilience and a growing wisdom to accept the fall outs and to seek friends that make them happy without complications.

I found it interesting as a principal that parents would naturally worry when their child transferred to our school, as they were concerned about how they would settle and make friends. In almost all cases, not only did their child settle, but they quickly learned how they were successful in forming new friendships. This undoubtedly built their self-esteem. The change of experience helped accelerate a better understanding of groups and friends.

Consider the following thoughts to support your child through the rigour of finding friends:

- Remember, *they're not your friends* and even though a child may choose a friend that you have some doubts about, it's important that they work out the ups and downs of that relationship. You're there to discuss their journey of friendship but you can't choose their friends.

- Take care not to talk negatively about their friends. This will confuse your child, and they will stop talking to you about them.

- Instead, encourage your child to talk openly about their friendship experiences. When they invite you to offer opinions, talk generally about what works in a friendship and perhaps talk about the highs and lows of your journey with friends.
- Be open and invite their friends to your house no matter what you may think about their suitability. In this area you should have an all-inclusive policy.
- Take care when having birthday parties. Ensure that it's an inclusive list where no one is left out.
- If your child talks about school related friendship issues, talk to the teacher with your child so that strategies can be put in place.
- A careful 'I' statement when a child talks about another child who has been unkind is worthwhile. For example:

> *'It sounds like they're not ready to be a good friend at the moment. I understand how you must feel about this.'*

> *Take care here not to talk negatively about the other child.*

- Never understate your child's upset feelings about failed relationships. They often feel this way because it affects their sense of self-worth.

Finally, a child must grow to own the responsibility of being in relationship with others. Parents can be great listeners, but children must experience the journey of learning about a relationship with all its disappointments and joys by themselves.

When things aren't smooth sailing

As the prep year turns into a few weeks, sometimes situations change for children. The friendship they thought was solid can shift, or perhaps someone acted inappropriately in the schoolyard. This can lead to hurt feelings and broken friendships. There are many small factors that can suddenly turn a sunny situation into feelings of sadness.

Children need to learn to adjust to changing scenarios. It's early days of building resilience in a child, developing emotional intelligence and building social literacies. Parents can suddenly feel anxious when what seemed a perfect start turns into their child not wanting to go to school. This sounds dramatic, but the turnaround in the child's mood can happen quickly and dramatically.

What a parent will do now is critical in showing their child how to deal with school issues.

Here are some easy steps to follow:

- Listen to their concerns.
- Show empathy but recognise when it's a problem that needs the teacher.
- Try and get your child to articulate their problem to the teacher.

Sometimes this doesn't work subject to the child's emotional maturity. Once the teacher knows the concerns, they will work with your child on the problem.

Tap in with your child along the way asking, 'How's the problem going?' Remember, we're teaching them that from an early age they own their issues and with support they can find solutions.

Don't forget to affirm your child once the problem is solved. For example:

> *'Well done. I'm proud that you worked out that problem with help from those that you trust.'*

Tests

Who likes being evaluated? Not many of us, from my understanding of human nature. Yet we regularly do this to children in schools across their school life.

Regular testing is considered necessary to further guide teaching for quality and in targeting the specific needs of your children. This is a valid reason but, for some children, the fear of regular assessment at school can have an impact on their sense of self-worth. It can also lower their interest in school and make them question their capacity to be successful.

If your child is inclined to feel anxious about testing, consider the following tips to help ease their worries:

- Make an appointment to talk to the teacher about the purpose of testing. This can help you understand why it might be important as a teaching tool. The teacher needs this information to guide their work. Progressive testing is a significant tool in teaching.

- Discuss with your child how you approached testing at school and what best helped you cope.
- Talk about how a test helps you learn what you need to know. For example:

> *'You got some of the words incorrect in this spelling test. That's actually good because now we know which words to work on!'*

- Some parents like to talk about tests as time to look for growth curves. For example:

> *'Well done. What directions do you need to take after that test?'*

- Talk about how successful a child is because they did the test, regardless of their results. The result is just to guide further teaching and learning.
- Don't focus on the detail of the test, especially the numeric results. Talking about the results – for example, seven out of ten – isn't as important as talking about what the child will work on from the results of the test.
- Talk about famous people who learnt from many trial and error experiments. Teachers will often talk to the class about how well-known sportspeople and scientists all tested their performance.

Ultimately, tests can cause increased anxiety in some children. A normal amount of anxiety is acceptable and can often drive better performance. However, should a child develop anxiety that is debilitating, this must be addressed with the school and home working together. Without collective understanding and support, it can lead to children refusing to be assessed.

There is no escaping the rigours of life which do come with assessments of all kinds. Here we're building a child's understanding of the value of testing and how it leads to further growth. It's all about measuring how far they've come and not what hasn't yet been learned. It's all about celebrating success to date and the effort put into the process of learning and growing.

> *'Success is a journey, not a destination. The doing is often more important than the outcome.'*
> **– Arthur Ashe**

Make the most of your mistakes

We all make mistakes and thank God for that!

Einstein was famous for commenting on how repeated mistakes led to his final discoveries. We need error to check our thinking and stimulate us to look for other ways and processes to be successful. Having said that, it's still often a concern for some children when they make a mistake, and some children can develop a fear of making a mistake.

When working with children, it often appeared to be tied up with their belief that they would let their parents down. Unfortunately, the more they're conditioned to hanging onto this fear, the less they'll try as they feel more secure in not trying at all. After all, that makes them feel more secure, but not for long!

Teachers often struggle with this issue in the classroom. We need to understand that the fear is rooted in disappointing others. Therefore, as I've mentioned throughout this book, we need to reassure them it's about 'having a go'.

Here are some suggestions for supporting your child through this fear of making mistakes:

- As a family, set up a 'having a go' sheet. Every time your child tells you that they really had a go over a tricky situation, put a tick on the sheet and agree to a reward when the chart has completed ten ticks. This shows that you're affirming their effort.
- Be spontaneous and, when you notice an attempt, affirm your child.
- When you look at the schoolwork that comes home, take care to comment on the work completed and the effort made. Avoid highlighting the mistakes.

    Here you would say:

> *'These comments by the teacher are where you can learn more. We all need to do this.'*

Talk about your own growth curves that you're working on to improve yourself.

- When chatting with your child across the week, talk about one situation where you 'had a go' even though it was hard. Discuss how you felt. You could say:

> *'I love your efforts. You always have a go and that's what I love about you.'*

Ten tips to support your child at school

Lastly, follow these tips to ensure that both you and your child feel supported during the primary years:

1. Ensure your child has plenty of sleep. This gives them the best start to stay focused during the day.
2. Consider your child's diet for lunch and snacks: not too heavy and low in sugar and wrap food in a way that is easy for your child to unravel.
3. Have a presence of school at home. This could be notes on fridges, awards on walls, diary dates included in family calendars and so on. The more your child feels that home connects to the school, the better.
4. Discuss the school uniform (if applicable) and what day they wear their sports gear. Discuss their involvement in getting ready each morning.
5. Read some of the school newsletters to them. This gives them a chance to talk to you about school events that affect them directly.
6. Don't ask too many questions at the beginning of the year. This can be overwhelming, as children think they need to have positive answers. Wait until they talk to you about their school day. Keep reinforcing how much you value their teacher. They like being reassured that their home and school is strongly connected.
7. Try to arrive at school on time or at least a few minutes early. This gives your child a chance to chat with their teacher about any pressing issues on their mind. It's also important to give children a sense

of continuity and to let them know that you value the importance of being on time. Children can feel uncomfortable walking into classrooms late. Further, always reassure your child that you will pick them up and on time. This reminder gives them an added sense of security, as the school days can be long.

8. Involve the whole extended family in positive and proud discussion about your child's school. Young children like to feel that school is valued by those that are close to them.

9. Be in touch – teachers need to be aware of any changes in family life. This is important given the impact that family life can have on a successful school environment. When a teacher notices some change in your child, they will often check in with you to establish if something has happened at home.

10. Developing independence – independent research indicates that the more children grow in independence, the greater capacity they have to learn. Giving greater independence to children can be difficult for some parents. But giving gradual independence is a comfortable way to support the growing child.

Chapter 21

Being in partnership with the school

School communication is the key

In my experience, when families are in a strong and trusting relationship with the school, children feel secure and happy.

Here are some suggestions for a strong relationship:

- Ensure that the class teacher knows who the immediate members of your child's extended family are.
- Ensure that contact emergency numbers are accurate and updated when necessary.
- When significant events occur in your family, especially if it causes anxiety for your child, please inform your teacher.
- Ensure that the school knows when your child will be absent. You should phone the office to advise of your child's absence and the office staff will notify the classroom teacher. This can also be done in advance via a note to the teacher.
- Please ensure any envelopes sent to the school are clearly marked with your child's name, class and subject.

- Talk to staff and ensure all your questions are answered. Staff will respond to emails. It's most important to ask the questions rather than build up anxiety about what you don't know.
- Assist your child with homework requirements. This doesn't mean doing the homework yourself, but it may involve rearranging life after school to ensure they have enough time to do homework.
- Where possible, connect your child's learning at school to family events.
- There are several groups or associations for parents that operate within a school and it's worth joining them.

School grounds gossip

Have you ever felt uncomfortable when you hear gossip around the school grounds? Unfortunately, this can be a common feature. School communities can be an environment that occasionally breeds unfortunate talk around the school grounds. However, you'll see teachers and the principal smiling and engaging with everyone first thing in the morning and after school to ensure a positive environment.

It's important to remember when we engage in conversation that has negative undertones and can include conversation about other people, your child will easily pick up the tone of the conversation and interpret it in their own way. They will be curious about your thoughts and beliefs and sometimes they'll carry this into the classroom and into their relationships.

Children value, want and actually expect your approval of their school environment. They become confused when they hear negative talk regarding their teacher, school mates and school community. Children struggle to understand the full context of what an adult conversation is about, especially if it's incidentally conducted, and so they may only hear aspects that unsettle them. I recommend that when talking with other families on school premises, take care to talk positively and to later reinforce to your child the positive aspects of your conversation.

If you're unsettled about any information or discussion your child has overheard, reassure them that you always seek clarification with the teacher or principal. Keep in mind that the school occupies a very big part of a child's life and it needs to be an emotionally safe place in which to work and play. A child needs to feel that their parents trust all aspects of school life and this is demonstrated by how they engage with the school over the year. Should unsettling conversations occur, then a child needs to understand that the best approach that's taken by their parents is to be in touch with the school.

There are many lessons to be learned in attending school and not all of them are in the classroom. One important lesson for our children is to understand how to be a community member and how to make positive connections with others no matter how different or challenging they may be. Children observe their parents' behaviour around the school environment; the more they show a positive disposition by engaging with the school optimistically, the more trusting and confident the child will be when they come to engage with school in different ways.

'Being positive in a negative situation isn't naïve.'
— **Ralph Watson**

Confidentiality in a school setting

Throughout your time at school, information will be gathered concerning enrolment data and educational information about your child. Confidentiality is a critical part of this, and schools respect all information that parents provide.

From time to time, extra information may be gathered regarding a child's learning. This is stored in a secure place and is only accessible to appropriate teachers and the principal. Records of children leaving the school are securely archived and are the school's responsibility.

It's part of every school's mandate to ensure confidentiality is strong. It's written across many of the school's policies and is a key feature of the school's code of conduct. Each year teachers are professionally guided in ensuring confidentiality is maintained as an important part of their work.

Chapter 22

The school year

What's in a school year

There are four terms in a school year. Each with its own character.

A teacher thinks and plans across four terms, each with ten weeks of work. As parents, you'll soon get into a similar routine of planning around the four terms and school holidays.

- **Term one** is all about establishment by building relationships, getting to know the children in class and forming friendship groups. Some children aren't great agents of change and settling in can take a little time. For some children, it may take the whole term, especially if they bonded well with their previous teacher and class. Teachers are settling into routine and it's important that parents understand how the teachers work. This way, you can best support your child by talking to them about their teacher's style.

- **Term two** is when routines and expectations are very clearly set. This is a time to ensure your child has established patterns of working at home and at school. It's most important that by this stage they are well settled into their class.

- **Term three** is serious consolidation and, by this time, teachers have a lot of data about their students where they set goals very specifically for each child. This is also wintertime and it's not uncommon for children to have bouts of illness. Keep an eye on their health and make sure they get plenty of sleep.
- **Term four** is a happy one and a time to really deepen their connections with teachers and the rest of the class. Towards the end of the year, anxiety can creep in with the prospect of change. This is a time to chat to them about the excitement of change and remind them how they settled into their current class earlier in the year.

Remember, school is about routine and each term has its own purpose and dynamic. At the commencement of the school year, the calendar of events is distributed to families.

By checking your family calendar with the school calendar, you can ensure there are no clashes which can sometimes unsettle your child if they miss important school events.

Getting back to school after holidays

Holidays are fun and take families away from routine which enables families to rest, talk more and engage in fun activities. It's all about the importance of slowing down, gathering around the table and just being family.

However, returning to school can often be unsettling for children. Consider having a family meeting and talk about what the school week will look like. Perhaps put a chart on the fridge outlining the plan for the next few weeks and ask your child to be part of this plan. If there will be variations to the weekly routine, ensure you let your child know well in advance as they can be part of all family movements.

Chat about what will be happening at school and ask your child if they know of any major events coming up. Re-establishing friendships for children can be a big issue, so you could generally talk about their friends to ensure their feeling comfortable about the change.

It's all about getting the routines slowly up and running. Enabling your child to be part of that plan and celebrating routine as a way of life in your family is important. A good start to the term sets the scene for a successful term overall.

Who are your best friends at school? The office team of course!

Schools are busy places and some of the best people for you to get to know are the office team; I speak now as a principal who relied heavily on my office staff for support.

They have such an excellent understanding of people's needs and are always the first to let the principal know if someone requires extra support. They're extremely intuitive to the needs of the whole school community.

They keep well briefed with the principal and are sometimes much easier to access than the school leaders. They're also very reliable to pass messages onto others.

Once office staff are familiar with you and the family, they're very conscious to support you when you need to learn more about the school or simply to get some facts straight. Office staff know to be extremely confidential and will point you in the right direction when you have specific inquiries.

I often think that the engine of a school is the office team. Keep them in mind as your support team when your child is at school. They play a critical role in the day-to-day life of the principal and the entire school community.

> *'Science and technology revolutionise our lives, but memory, tradition and myth frame our response.'*
> **– Arthur M Schlesinger**

Chapter 23

Good habits

Keeping school attendance consistent

I certainly don't want to sound like the punitive principal who stresses the need to be consistent with school attendance. However, there are reasons why being consistent in attending school is so important for your child's overall development.

Firstly, children need to develop the lifelong habit of getting up and being accountable to something important and, in this case, attending school. It's about having a purpose for getting up. Children are keen to be punctual for sporting events or other exciting events where they feel strongly connected to their peers and the activity. While school may not have that same buzz each day, the habit of getting up and regularly attending school teaches them that they are honouring an important responsibility – consistent learning.

Behavioural changes can happen if a child has protracted absences from school. They feel anxious about returning as they worry about friendship groups moving on from them. Missing out on schoolwork also causes them to feel less successful in learning and this can cause other problems such as disinterest in their work or a general lack of motivation.

In order for children to enjoy school, they need to feel successful socially and in their schoolwork. Frequent absences diminish their capacity to be successful on both levels.

It's also apparent that when children return to school after absences of any length, sometimes their behaviour might change as they're feeling unsure of themselves and their place amongst their peers. Teachers will often comment on the noticeable change.

Another important reason for regular attendance is that you're giving them a strong message that learning is an important part of their life and that you value their attendance each day.

If there are significant reasons for absences including sickness or family holidays, discuss with your child why it's important to be absent and plan with the school how you'll manage the situation as a family. By doing this, you're telling your child that you respect the role of school in their life.

I appreciate that for some children a week at school can be a long time. It's approximately five hours a day and children have set expectations across that time. Now consider school across ten weeks of a term and forty weeks across the year. This can be a big demand for some children who feel the pressure to succeed or who struggle with peer relations. However, allowing them to stay at home for indefinite periods only heightens their anxiety.

If school refusal creeps in, parents should act quickly and talk to the school. You should also give your child reassurance at home that you're proud of their efforts and I would suggest listing the positives you notice about school. Should your child start rejecting school, you must act quickly: the sooner it's understood, and support is given, the quicker your child can move on from being anxious.

Schools are well supported when it comes to helping children settle into school. Keep the school in the loop as they take their responsibility very seriously with regard to children's well-being.

Schools become a way of life for the family. The more a child embraces this way of life, the better opportunities are there to develop into a lifelong learner.

Simple tools to ease the stress of homework

Do you have a regular homework time set aside in your house? Homework time can be difficult, as each child will often have different expectations on how to do homework and when to do homework, if at all! Homework is often done at the busiest and most tiring part of the day, after school and around dinner time.

If you find homework time challenging, here are six tips that may ease the pressure:

1. Have a box of goodies set up. This means that the box contains pencils, pens and Textas which your child can easily access to start their homework straight away. I've heard of some parents providing little treats in the box as they dig around for their necessary tools. This makes it fun!

2. Set up a visible roster – perhaps on the fridge – outlining homework tasks and on what day they'll be done. As a family, agree that they'll be done on that day.
3. Recognise at what time homework should finish, as extended time on homework is usually ineffective. If the homework is too difficult, or your child doesn't understand it, agree as a family to discuss it with the teacher in the morning and no further time is wasted on it.
4. If your child is spending too much time on a task and you've attempted to help unsuccessfully, this can give them a sense of failure and it actually becomes quite unproductive for your relationship. Best to stop!
5. The family should all agree on where the best place is to do homework. I would recommend that it's visible to you, although too much supervision takes ownership from your child. Settle on a place that has few distractions, is comfortable and has plenty of light. Keep the area uncluttered as this creates the impression that homework is the focus and there is no distraction. Consider the surrounding noise levels.
6. Is it possible that your child does their homework in the morning after breakfast and before school? Children are more attentive and learn more effectively when refreshed after sleep.

Finding a balanced dose of media

Do you often have a panic wondering if your children have been watching too much television or using their technology for too long? I imagine this can happen when pressure on family life varies; it's difficult to find consistency in a busy world.

However, it's important to find the right balance with media and technology use, as excessive screen time can limit a child's ability to converse, engage with other activities and it reduces reading hours and listening capacity.

Here are some suggestions for trying to find the balance with use of technology at home:

- Look at the week ahead. Does it have a balanced approach after school?
- Are their certain television programs that your child enjoys? Perhaps negotiate with your child when they watch television in the light of all the other chores and homework required for that week.
- Talk about the programs they enjoy watching on television. Find out what really interests your child in these programs and other interactive games. Don't forget to always monitor the ratings.
- Be a positive role model. Reduce your own personal time on the computer and watching television, replacing them with family talk time or active family activities. Your child needs to see that there are other important ways of operating as a family.
- Technology is embedded in our world and especially your child's life. Talk about how they enjoy technology and discuss and research together the various ways in which technology has impacted the world. By doing this, your child can reflect on the technological impact over the years. At the same time, they can reflect on the importance of other

aspects of life that can't be neglected; these are enlivening experiences that are not technologically driven.

- Introduce house rules about where computers are kept and where charging spots are located. Take control of all technology, thereby making it easy and visible to access for yourself. Bedrooms are notorious hiding spaces for children in which to overuse computers.

Schools are constantly evaluating the use of technology in the classrooms. We've moved on from believing that technology will drive every moment of our school day to recognising that children need to learn in different ways and that excessive dependence on technology diminishes a child's capacity to think and process. For example: teamwork, group discussions and cooperative learning doesn't rely on technology. A child needs varied cooperative models of learning.

When planning family holidays, consider having them without technology. For example, go camping or hiking. Outdoor activities are wonderful for taking the mind off technology. Children need to learn life in ways not driven by an iPad!

There are some wonderful websites which teach the family about cyber safety, such as the Government's E-Safety websites (www.esafety.gov.au and https://aifs.gov.au/search/site/cyber) and the Bravehearts website (https://bravehearts.org.au/what-we-do/education-and-training/for-parents/keeping-safe-online/). I recommend looking at these with your child as it gives you both important ideas and issues to discuss.

Also learn about how to take authority in blocking certain social media. Websites such as Victoria Police's online safety website (https://www.police.vic.gov.au/online-safety) have excellent advice in this area. Talk to your child's school about what they're teaching the children with regard to cyber safety. They often send excellent support material home to families. Schools also hold information nights about home use of technology.

Remember, we live in a technologically driven world which has an extraordinary capacity to influence our lives. Our children are embedded with the notion that living with technology is a natural process. What we should do as parents is applaud the inevitable but put on the table all the options of enjoying and savouring life with and without technology. We remind ourselves that our children have been born into a totally different time. What a difference a generation makes!

Home is a great place to start reading

Parents have a huge influence on their children. Teachers often comment on how children repeat what their parents say, show mannerisms like them or they frequently talk about their parents.

One of the most valuable things a parent can do as a role model is to read with them.

Research tells us that early reading with children has a significant influence on the development of their speech, how they interact with parents and it sharpens their auditory skills.

I recommend leaving picture books scattered around the house and having special reading times together. Share the reading together at night. Reading together can be so much fun and a chance to spend further quality time together.

If your child sees that you value reading, they will also value reading.

Your example has an impact on your child.

PART 4

Anxiety

Chapter 24

The sources of anxiety

Be alert but not alarmed ... the quiet child

Quiet children are clever. In some cases, they've learned to not discuss their issues at home. There can be a variety of reasons for this, but one reason, which is evident through observation, is that sometimes parents are great talkers with strong personalities, and the child can't compete. They also feel safe as they don't have the chance to say the wrong thing.

When you listen to your child, be still and give eye contact. This gives them emotional space to process their thoughts. Talking to them with a gentle and calm voice reassures them that there will be no consequences to what they say and how they say it. Often, finding a quiet space gives your child more opportunities to talk about their day.

I recently walked past a group of boys very actively engaged in conversation with each other. As I turned to notice them, I was surprised that the ringleader, who had much to say, was a little boy who usually doesn't talk much with his family. In fact, he was receiving counselling for being quiet and reserved. He smiled at me looking somewhat coy and said, 'Yes, Mrs Smith. See, I can talk when I want to'.

Children engage with us better if they aren't overwhelmed by our style of parenting or expect a reaction. Gentle always wins the day.

Keeping an eye on the quiet child

Do you have a quiet child? They might be the one who sits and listens more or perhaps just responds to questions with one-word answers. They might be the child that doesn't want to stand out in a crowd or appears happy to follow others in various activities. In every classroom there will be those children who won't make their presence felt or who enjoy being part of a group in a non-distinguishable way.

Many people are quiet, shy or timid in their approach to communication with others. While this is an acceptable trait, it's still worth monitoring children who appear exceptionally quiet or disinterested in engaging with others. There could be many reasons why remaining quiet and unnoticed is a preferred option for some children.

While a child is developing intellectually, physically, emotionally and socially, this is the time to encourage them to be comfortable and confident in speaking out. They need to develop their voice, feel it's heard and gain success from someone's response. If a child remains too silent, they can build up resentment and feel frustrated that they're not achieving success like other children. They will become conditioned into operating this way which becomes an accepted pattern of communicating where everyone around them adjusts to their silence.

It's also important to encourage a quiet child into conversation as they can become quite dependent on their silence which acts as a defence mechanism by avoiding social issues. We need our children to deal with issues, problems or conflicts that arise using language with growing confidence. In today's world where we're very aware of child safety, we need to give our children confidence that their voice is heard and valued. They need to feel that using their voice is another way of being safe.

When working with children, I was especially aware that when talking to a quiet child I needed to ask very open-ended questions. I also needed to speak in a quiet and comforting voice that didn't take over the conversation. If at any point I spoke as though I was in charge of the conversation, they simply wouldn't engage.

Here are a few tips on how to encourage a quiet child to use and strengthen their voice:

- When talking as a family unit, check in with your quiet child by asking questions that don't give them any distress, especially when in front of other members of the family.
- Ask and state open-ended questions or statements, not closed ones. For example:

> 'Tell me some happy things that happened at school today.'

Some families have starter up sentences which they play as a family. For example:

> 'Today I went to the park and ...'
> 'I like breakfast because ...'

This can be turned into a fun activity. The principle here is to encourage longer responses to the statement.

- Affirm your child when they give you a sound explanation. For example:

  'Thanks for telling me that story.
  You explained it so well.'

- Writing stories and reading them out aloud is another way of a child hearing their voice and others responding to it through questioning and affirming.
- Take care not to dominate a conversation. This can be easily done as quiet children will simply let you keep on with the conversation. Retreating into silence is not an acceptable response.

These are a few strategies you can use to help encourage quiet children to give them confidence and to use the power of their voice.

Be alert to trauma in children

Every childhood experience has an impact on the body and mind and some more lasting and meaningful than others.

Sometimes due to circumstances that may be out of your control as parents, your child may experience severe trauma. This could be because of a divorce in the family, death of a parent or grandparent, an accident and so on. I won't discuss the nature of the trauma, rather, I'll discuss how to understand and manage the trauma. Once trauma occurs, a child may have difficulties coping in a range of areas which might surprise parents.

Their brain is busy coping with the experience of trauma and, as such, their ability to learn at a normal pace, socialise effectively and respond to life will generally have its limitations. It's as though their whole world is dulled. Sometimes when family trauma occurs, parents can worry about their child's school performance and inability to show interest in activities that they usually love. It's quite acceptable to allow a child the emotional space to recover from the trauma. We need to accept that performance will naturally drop off for a while. It's important to let this happen so that your child can recover from the shock and get back their resources slowly. Take care not to place too many expectations on them during this recovery phase.

When a child has such an experience, they need space from what they normally engage in so that they can recover their body and mind's demands. I've seen children stop reading after trauma occurs. I myself stopped reading at the age of seven when my parents divorced.

Children can also slow down their speech and hear words but not comprehend what's said. I've also seen children needing much more sleep, stuttering and losing their skills and interest in formal games. Younger children sometimes wet the bed. Their resilience to others deteriorates. This is just a short list of how trauma can manifest itself in a child's behaviour. If this happens to your child, be prepared to allow them the space and time to process the trauma. Understand that providing a climate where they can simply 'be' without pressure is the best healing space for them. With sensitive support and strong nurture, your child will recover.

The brain is an extraordinary muscle. It goes into overload when trauma occurs and shutting down in certain areas is a way for the brain to rest, regroup and prepare to heal. Allowing a child that space is critical for effective recovery. It's not a time to work on improving performance or increasing the workload to keep up to standard. Most likely, work performance will deteriorate.

For parents, it's a time to respect and appreciate a child's recovery time which will vary in length from child to child.

*'Trauma is a fact of life.
It does not however have to be a life sentence.'*
– Peter A Levine

When separation occurs

These are tricky times for everyone when this happens.

It's natural to get caught up with your own emotional roller coaster and reflecting on your child's emotional state can be secondary. Often, a child will go quiet when separation occurs. In their minds they are waying up how they're valued in their parents' eyes.

A child will often become worried that if one parent has gone, will they lose the other parent? This was quite common in discussions with children going through a family separation. Their sense of being valued seemed at risk.

Given that they become emotionally anxious, it was also common for children to slip back academically and to feel socially less secure. A child looks carefully for signs of reassurance from parents when family circumstances change.

I appreciate that the above sounds daunting. However, with careful planning and engaging your child in the transformation of the family, they come through with a reassured sense of their place in the new structures of the family.

Here are some suggestions to help with the journey of separation:

- Keep your child in the loop – but within reason. There isn't anything more insecure for a child than not being aware of what's really happening. Being honest is very important to your child, they'll look for information elsewhere if they're not being given the truth. They'll also imagine the worst if they're unsure about their position in the family.

- Remember that a child loves both parents and no matter how you feel toward your ex-partner, to your child, they're still very important in their life. How you manage this is an individual family matter. The important factor here is to remember that your child has a totally different perspective of their other parent than you.

- Speak gently to your child about why the relationship has broken down. They don't need to hear and feel the hostility or anger you might feel yourself.

- Investing in a counsellor is very helpful as it gives your child the opportunity to talk independently to someone they trust. It enables them to express their feelings which can be difficult in the home setting for fear of upsetting parents.

In my experience, if a parent's behaviour is quite reactive and volatile, the child will go quiet and shut down. Being silent can mean that they're not coping with the situation.

There are some excellent children's books on separation and divorce. These are wonderful to read together in a safe and happy space.

Choose your time wisely when talking to your child about the separation. If you're not feeling up to it, then delay the chat. It's better to have quality time together than broken and unsettling conversations.

Remember, it's important for a child to feel happy. Even though life is tough, remember to play, laugh and enjoy your child.

As custody orders come into the business of separation and divorce, take care to ensure that what's arranged is the least unsettling for your child. Include them in making decisions about what to pack and where to meet the other parent. They need to take some ownership of this process over time. This gives them more personal security.

Be careful with idle and loose conversations around your child. Children are particularly sensitive to conversations around them when they're feeling vulnerable.

The age of your child when the separation occurs is important to understand how your sensitive talk goes with them. A younger child should be spoken to very gently, calmly and not in long protracted explanations. They will catch onto what you say and feel the anxiety very quickly.

Remember, that as the child grows with the separation, they'll need to keep understanding how they fit into shifting family arrangements. This is especially the case when new partners enter the relationship, or a parent goes through significant changes in their life.

Their journey in the family split is quite different from your experience, and they'll understand and reflect on it from different perspectives as they grow older. Their grief is also different and so we need to respect their right to travel through the journey of separation in their own way and in their own time.

Body image

There's so much that needs to be said around this and it can't all be said in one small section of this book. However, there is one valuable point that I wish to bring to parents' attention. This is based on my considerable experience as a school principal and also experience as parent and grandparent.

As children grow, they're exposed to their own physical changes. This is natural. Their peers and the other people around them will also talk about their changing shapes. All of this is to be expected and parents can't stop the chatter that goes on around body image.

So, join it!

One great support in reducing anxiety in this area is to engage your children in active sports over their growing years. The more a child's interest grows with being physically stronger, the more they'll develop a positive body image that is built around being healthy and productive. I've seen this time and time again. I noticed that children who loved and gravitated around sports were more inclined to associate with children who had similar interests. Their conversations were about building strong bodies to do better times on the track, in the pool, on the waves, on the basketball court and so on. They developed a stronger self-awareness of body image and were more educated and interested in learning how healthy bodies worked. They were also given supportive advice through clubs and training sessions and enjoyed talking about how to improve their stamina.

I've seen this in my own children – and now grandchildren – who are keen to associate with like-minded children who talk about feeling good as being more important as looking good. The self-discipline they gain from being part of teams and the social comradery protects them from the murky world of social media and 'looking pretty'. To them, being attractive is tied up with a having a healthy body that works well.

My recommendation is simple. Involve the children in organised sport from an early age. This may mean exploring different sports until you choose one that provides an environment in which you feel happy and secure as you'll be handing your children over to coaches and other supportive parents on a regular basis. There is often a like mindedness in these clubs and this continues to support healthy images about bodies. There is also strong role modelling from parents who have a love for being fit themselves. One warning! Ensure the club is a positive one promoting competition on a healthy level.

Once your child sees their body as something that is beautiful by nature of being healthy and fit, they'll be comfortable in their own skin and steer away from the shady world of social media presenting warped and tailored images.

'Just play. Enjoy the game. Have fun.'
– Michael Jordan

Chapter 25

Parents and their children's anxiety

Do we worry about our children becoming anxious?

Some parents become quite concerned about their child having some anxiety and often work in overdrive to take it all away. Sadly, as school principal, I came across some situations where parents wouldn't send their children to school on certain days if they felt anxious about things such as friendships issues, tests, sports day and so on. In the case of visiting elderly homes – a common excursion in schools – a few parents didn't want their children to visit them in case it upset their child seeing an old person who may die.

A big discussion in education is the business of sport and rewarding children for winning in competitive sport. However, some schools have opted to only distribute involvement ribbons so that children won't be upset about not winning.

And so, the debate rages in education about the value of rewarding success over effort. This isn't about finding the right solution to the debate but, rather, I suggest that some anxiety is good for a child. Call it a necessary growth curve. Children need to be exposed to different opportunities in order to work through some anxiety. This often includes giving them more independence – certainly, more emotional independence. You need to give your child the skills to work through the anxiety.

To help them through their anxiety, you could say:

> *'It seems that you feel a little anxious about the test today. Good luck. You're making the effort which is success in itself.'*

> *'Good luck in the race. I'm so pleased you're having a go. Well done."*

Your child might not win the race, but they'll feel better for exposing themselves to the process. Being part of the race gives them a feeling of involvement and achievement.

Bring them into a situation so that they feel connected to the journey. If, for example, you child attends an excursion to an aged care facility you could say:

> *'Today, I hear you're visiting an aged facility to visit older people. You'll see many people who are struggling with their health and age. This is a normal part of growing older.'*

If your child becomes attached to a resident who, over several visits, happens to pass on, consider the empathy and understanding they develop for life and the awareness of accepting and seeing difference. Yes, they'll have had anxiety about the situation, but they'll come out the experience richer and emotionally stronger. Their understanding of life has grown. Avoiding anxious moments that are within reason only delays growth.

Anxiety will keep appearing and throughout life the later we get to manage it, the more difficult it is to recover. Children are very aware of differences and this is obvious as early as prep when they begin to read. They see that some children are better than them.

You might notice their awareness of not reading as well as other children. You can say:

> 'I love the fact that you try so hard with your reading.
> Every time you read; you're getting better.'

Your child will need to accept differences and appreciate and value their own capabilities which also comes with limits.

A few final tips to help you support your children dealing with mild anxiety:

- Talk to your child about the things that make you anxious and tell them about the strategies you use to help work on the problem.
- Talk about anxiety as being part of life. We have it in many forms; from rushing to work to be on time, to more anxious moments of performance in races, tests and work.
- Talk positively about how a child manages their anxiety. For example:

> *'It sounds like you have to sing in the concert and, of course, you feel nervous. Well done for all the effort in practising. This is a great way to get ready for your performance.'*

- Read stories to your child on how others overcame struggles and anxiety.
- Point out public figures (choose wisely) who have worked hard to overcome their anxieties. Children love hearing about heroes. They enjoy identifying with others who have worked on their anxieties and improved their emotional stamina.

Finally, a child who has success in working through mild anxieties is more resilient when bigger anxieties come their way. They develop a set of skills that give them the strength to work through issues.

Feeling sorry is important – but within reason

Do you have a very sensitive child? If so, you'll understand how sometimes they'll disproportionately worry or feel upset. Do you have a child always apologising or perhaps getting upset very easily over minor situations?

Here I'll discuss putting worries into proportion. I recently heard a psychologist talk about how something she experienced as a child stayed with her for a very long time. She had deep feelings of regret and sorrow over something that wasn't seen in the correct light or understood by adults. It was a displaced issue where someone in the family had died but she had not seen them for a while and, as a small child, she felt some responsibility for their passing. This might sound a crazy connection, but sometimes a child's mind can carry that sad feeling into adulthood. This silence can be deafening as the years progress.

Think about your own childhood. Were there any incidents that you can recall that brings sadness to your mind and where you blame yourself? Often, families separating when a child is young can stay with a child into adulthood. The question they might have is: 'Was I to blame? If only I'd done something about it.'

These irrational sorrows can subliminally linger in our minds for quite some time. When working with children, I was always keen to clear the cobwebs and I'd invite children to talk about their fears and worries.

Here are some tips to keep children's worries up on the surface of their thoughts and not buried deep to be resurrected as an adult:

- As a family, plan weekly chats about everyone's week. Use this occasion to talk about family issues that have been dealt with and discuss how everyone feels about them.
- If you notice your child not talking about something, find a quiet time to chat with them. It's best to deal with it sooner rather than later.
- Use the scale system. On a scale of one to ten, how did our week go? Be honest about situations that you had to deal with and chat about how you felt at the time.
- At the end of the week, reflect on issues and situations that may have impacted on your child. This gives you the chance to sensitively discuss

them as a family. Teaching children that regularly talking about feelings is a positive and emotionally settling thing to do.

A child will understand problems subject to their age and how it's understood in the family. This is about teasing out any unsettling situations or issues that might be locked into their minds.

Of course, children should feel sorry over certain situations or issues, but it should be a mentally healthy way of being sorry.

Call it your weekly 'throw away the cobwebs' session.

It's common practice in classrooms to have a review session of the week where the teacher draws out issues, highlights and thoughts about the week just passed. This helps the children reflect on anything that has been unsettling and that needed an open discussion. Children look forward to this open discussion.

Power games can be dangerous

I've briefly mentioned the use of power throughout this book. This time I'll discuss how power can be hidden in how we communicate. We might be perfectly innocent about using power, but it still can appear in our behaviour. Sometimes children look for signs of their parents using too much power.

However, let's not get confused with authority. As parents, we have the responsibility to provide for our children and we have the authority to manage them. A child, as early as a pre-schooler, comes to know how you operate. They read the signs very well as they need to feel reassured that everything is okay with the relationship. In fact, they're frequently checking in with us to see how they're going in their parent's eyes.

These signs – through our behaviour – need to be positive, clear and consistent. Giving your child mixed messages only makes them anxious and confused and can be construed as use of power. Intermittent anxiety can be hard to live with because we have no prediction of how we'll react to certain situations.

The following are suggestions to keep your behavioural messages clear to your child:

- When you need to talk to a child about something, speak calmly and with clarity. Often, when a child is listening to the teacher about how they've done something wrong in class, they'll say that the teacher 'yelled' at them. *How* you speak to a child is important.
- Short sentences and breaks in between sentences help children better process what you're saying to them.
- Ensure the environment where you talk to a child is appropriate. Busy shopping centres, and noisy and crowded spaces will only make them feel overwhelmed by the situation and powerless to respond.

Also, as discussed throughout this book, remember to use the 'I' statement. For example:

'I'm disappointed that you ...'

Use the positive 'I' statement to also ensure balance in conversations. For example

'I'm very happy that you ...'

Ensure that your child understands your purpose for the conversation. Never let them hover around being unsure about the outcomes as this can be unsettling and can indirectly be seen as using power.

When talking to a child about something, remember to maintain eye contact and listen with care when they respond. Your child needs to feel that you're really listening to their response and that you value what they say. Always follow up after an issue has been resolved and affirm your child's efforts in working through situations.

The use of power over children eventually runs out as they grow, and they realise the empty vessel that power has become. We need to be developing a positive influence on our children so that they come to us unimpeded by fear of consequences. Teaching them how to manage themselves without relying on the use of power is the key.

When working with children, it wasn't uncommon for them to tell me which parents they would go to when a problem arose and, no surprises, that it was the parent that listened and didn't force their thinking onto them. The more balanced you are as a parent, the more comfortable your child will be. When talking with children as a principal, it was important for me to remember that my status as principal could be quite daunting for them. Care in my conversation with them was so crucial in ensuring the relationship was intact.

Children gravitate around what is mentally safe for them. They seek it out. They intuitively search for love and will be comfortably in tune with parents that they emotionally trust.

> *'Each day of our lives we make deposits in the memory banks of our children.'*
> **– Charles R Swindell**

How do *you* feel today?

As a parent, have you noticed that you can have many ups and downs? Mood swings can be common in most people and especially in parents who are always giving but not very often receiving in their family. Selflessness can be wearing and there are times that you must find personal space to recover from juggling work, home and family commitments.

Regulating our emotions is very important around our children. We need to understand our shifting emotional state and, that if we tend to get quite low, we need to have strategies to help us.

Do we recognise when we're in this state, especially for prolonged periods? Do we understand ourselves enough to know when our emotional reactions are too extreme in front of our children? Are we able to monitor this or are we struggling to regulate our emotions when dealing with family problems?

Too many extreme emotional swings can create anxiety in children.

I remember parents telling me that when they were overreactive regularly, they could see a confused look on their child's face and they would shut down. Children tend to retreat as a means of survival. Similarly, teachers know how quickly they can lose their student's approval when they're not in control.

The following are some tips to assist in monitoring your emotional response when around children:

- Always understand when you're tired. This will help you make decisions on how capable you are to have discussions about family matters that can be emotional.

- If there are issues that cause you considerable distress or anger, is it necessary for you to be part of that discussion? Can someone else close to your child take on that issue?

- Talk to your child about how you value regulating your emotions. Perhaps you have some strategies that they could adopt, such as taking big breaths before responding to a difficult situation, walking away, thinking positive thoughts and so on.

- If there are certain issues that really press your buttons, explain this to your child. If there are legitimate reasons as to why you can overreact easily, let them know these reasons.

- Remember that when you do overreact or become emotionally charged, always come back to your child with an apology or at least an explanation and let them know why you're disappointed in your overreaction. This demonstrates to your child that you're sincere in trying to regulate your emotions. After all, we are human!

Using some of these strategies tells your child that you value emotional balance in your life. It's important in taking ownership of yourself. This kind of modelling imprints on your child that working towards being in control is developing social and emotional maturity and should be valued.

As a principal, it was always a concern of mine that I acted in the same controlled way. Sometimes it wasn't easy, but it was necessary.

Watch out for the doubting Thomas in your child

It's quite natural to doubt yourself. However, children need to build their self-confidence and overall capacity, in whatever challenges them. This is an important part of parents' work, to reassure our children that they're capable beings and can develop the skills to rise above fears and doubts. We help them in many ways by reassuring them and praising them when they're successful.

While all of our encouragement is helpful and has value, it's also about giving children strategies to use when they feel doubtful. After all, we can reassure children that they're capable, but it's better in teaching them how to manage doubtful feelings once they recognise that they have them.

When you own the responsibility of taking control of your own feelings, you're more successful at managing them. It also brings greater satisfaction in the long run. When your child has doubts about their capabilities in some area, remind them that doubtful feelings are normal and that there are several ways to get on top of those feelings.

Firstly, ask your child to openly talk about their doubt. This is about bringing it out in the open for discussion. For example:

> *'I don't think I can pass that test.
> It'll be too hard.'*

Ask them to give the doubt feeling a number out of ten. Then talk about times when they had success and passed similar tests.

Now set a goal that is attainable, for example:

> *'I'll try to do my best so that I've had a go just
> like everybody else.'*

The idea is to get them thinking about achieving part of the goal. After the test, check in to see how the goal went and ask what number they would now give themselves when doubting themselves.

Another example is when a child thinks they can't run well in a race. What number do they give the doubt? Set a small goal. For example:

> *'I'll try my best and just get to the end.'*

It's all about setting small goals that help them begin to break down the doubt.

When working with children, it was quite common to discuss the degree of doubt they had and then set a small goal to chip away at the lack of confidence. It was always important to come back together and celebrate the child's achievements, no matter how small.

When we reassure our children of their capabilities, we teach them to manage their doubts. They are then better equipped to cope independently.

'Successful people have fears.

Successful people have doubts and successful people have worries.

They just don't let these feelings stop them.'
– T Harv Eker

Chapter 26

Practical ways to deal with anxiety

Children really enjoy using practical tools to help reflect on their feelings. They enjoy touching and feeling objects and working in practical ways. In this chapter, I'll outline some practical activities and strategies you can use to reduce anxiety in your child.

Weigh it up

Try using your scales at home and collect a few pebbles. When a child is chatting about their problems, they can put a pebble on the scale. For example:

> *'Hmm, is that a heavy problem?'*

As the pebbles mount, talk about how these problems can just weigh you down. Then invite them to talk about happy experiences that may lighten their load. Put these pebbles on the other side of the scale. Talk about times when they were able to solve their problems.

Sometimes just putting the pebbles on the problem side is enough. As you talk about what can take that problem away, you remove the pebbles and comment on how things seem lighter.

> *'It seems you worked out how to*
> *solve that problem.'*

When I've used this activity with children, they're often keen to paint faces on the rocks to express their feelings. This could be an activity to do with them before you use the scales.

There are many variations of this idea. For example, putting the rocks in a bag and just feeling the weight.

> *'Problems can be heavy, can't they?'*

The principle is about children reflecting on lightening their load. It's amazing how such a practical and simple activity can make a difference with younger children. In a child's mind, problems can mount throughout the week and can quickly seem insurmountable. Many of these problems can melt away quickly with such a simple activity and positive talk. Sometimes a child will just play with the rocks and talk about their problems. The more relaxed the talk, the better to deconstruct the problem.

Have fun with your child selecting some rocks or pebbles and these can be the tools you use to carry out this activity.

Have you ever sat down and played with sand?

We've found that children whose emotions rise high can easily calm down just by simply sitting and immersing themselves in sand. This is so successful in our school setting that many teachers request a sand tray for their classrooms! The therapy is effective and so easy to set up. Children who are angry need some support in regulating their emotions and the calm distraction of the sand tray works magic!

I would recommend having a sand tray at home, especially if you have a young child who can't articulate their feelings and who are prone to becoming angry very quickly. I find that as a child calms down, talking to them gently is a way for them to gradually talk about their frustrations and regulate their emotions. Playing with them in the sand tray also gives them a shared experience with you as the parent. Sand trays are particularly wonderful for children with ASD and who might have difficulty in expressing themselves. Sometimes a child will create images in the sand that express their feelings, and this makes it easier to talk specifically about their problems. Sometimes just simply playing with the sand is therapeutic and regulates high emotions.

A picture is worth a thousand words

Sometimes younger children struggle to understand how to deal with a situation that can overwhelm them. This could be about finding friends, or it could be trying to work out how to play with other children. One way to help a child is to simply draw the story. For example, how best to play with others. The first page shows your child meeting a friend. The second page may show them greeting the other child and the third page could be about what to say such as, 'Can I play with you?'

The story unfolds through the simple pictures. Keep the pictures and story simple. We call this a social story, and they work very well with children who can't respond well to being told what to do; some children don't process the problem easily through discussion.

I've used this with many children, and they love telling the story through the pictures. Children especially enjoy telling you how successful they were when they went through the process and followed the picture book. A social story can change if you find it needs a new direction.

Children learn through visual images and when they're emotional about something, pictures speak a thousand words. Simple drawings can say many unspoken words which gives a child the chance to express their feelings comfortably. To help a young child, parents can draw their own social story to help their child understand the value of the pictures.

What an image can tell us

One of my greatest tools when working with children is a chart that has faces on it that express different feelings. These faces include a range of feelings: happy, sad, joy, calm, anger, embarrassment and so on. Children love choosing one to talk about how they feel on that day. This is a wonderful way of engaging with them easily, as younger children often have difficulty expressing their feelings or are simply needing more time.

I have other more sophisticated charts to express feelings, but all our students choose the simpler, easy to translate chart. Parents may find such a chart a great tool at home in inviting children to talk about their emotions. It's visible, clearly understood and gives parents easy access to their child's emotions. These charts can be obtained in some news agencies or can be drawn up at home and laminated. Once again, this should be visible and an easy-to-understand way of expressing feelings.

Lock it up and forget about it

This is an activity to help children deal with mild anxieties.

I would only use this if the problem was a simple one. I've used this method with children who enjoy the practical act of locking up their problems and then throwing away the key. Great fun! A little bit of theatre is a good thing, and something that I'll further discuss later on in this chapter.

It's all about getting your child to imagine that the problem can't return and that they have control over managing the problem. It's all in our control and we choose to remove the problem.

I remember several years ago using this activity with a child. When I spoke to her as a teenager, she told me how she imagined locking away her problems and this strategy still helped her with issues. The key remained a big focus in her mind.

I've seen this work by writing the problem on a piece of paper and then either ripping it up or burying it. It's about finding a practical and reasonable way of disposing of the anxious thought. Children enjoy the game and throw themselves into the feeling of letting go of the anxiety.

Teachers often have quiet times where they simply invite the class to absorb their thoughts by focussing only on the positive. This helps children to slow down and put things into perspective.

It's only a balloon

Balloons can be lots of fun.

They're also easily available and can be great to express feelings.

For example, if your child has had a bad day, ask them to blow up the balloon thinking about all the things that went wrong. They can mention the issues or problems with each new breath taken. Then let it go! Wow, it splatters everywhere and, of course, makes the appropriate sound.

Then you can say, 'Problems are blown away into the air!'

Children can also draw a sad face on the balloon before they let it go.

I've used this with younger children, and they enjoy the experience of letting their sad feelings just blow away.

It's all about providing the experience that takes away the anxious feelings. Parents can experiment at home by using tools such as balloons or doing things like blowing out candles or sweeping away the cobwebs.

For those that like a touch of drama

This might not be for everyone but acting out situations can be a great way of telling stories and learning about feelings. When your child is feeling sad and you feel up to the exercise, try acting out a story that they're familiar with.

For example, act out the Three Little Pigs. Your child joins in and soon the attention goes to the drama and the story, and their attention is taken from their first preoccupations.

When the acting is over you can say:

*'You seemed sad before.
Are you feeling better now?'*

Another great example of acting out is through finger puppets. Children enjoy becoming the character and sometimes discuss their feelings through the puppets. I've seen this dramatic activity also done with plastic gloves where children draw the characters firstly on the fingers of the gloves.

Using drama is about transferring the feeling onto the character and talking through the emotions. I've always found that children who struggle to express themselves and don't feel confident around peers show a great interest in drama and often excel in this field. They thoroughly enjoy taking on another character and expressing them in a public way.

In fact, many famous actors started out as shy children and used drama as a way to talk about their feelings.

Reading through the problems

There are many beautiful books that are written for children to think through their problems.

They work well as children can see the problem as someone else's problem and, as the story unfolds and a solution is found, children can put themselves in the place of the character. Reading through the problem is a safe way of reflecting on and understanding how to manage their own feelings.

Remember, that when you read the story to your child, highlight how the character solved the problem and ask:

'Have you ever had that feeling yourself?'

Children are very familiar with using books to tell stories that have a message. Teachers use this method all the time to inform, teach and instruct. Remember, repeating the stories is also a good idea to reinforce the concepts and deepen their understandings, especially with younger children.

Librarians are great resources and can recommend excellent books to parents on various topics around feelings and emotions.

A little box with tricks inside

Parents often tell me that getting children to talk about their concerns is difficult. Some parents have found great success in using this idea.

Invite your child to decorate a small box – no bigger that a shoe box and even smaller is a good idea. Ask them to decorate it in a way that expresses themselves. Your child should keep the box in a special place in their room. When they feel they want to talk about a problem, suggest they write the problem down on paper and leave it in the box. At night, when you tuck them in ready to say goodnight, ask them if they would like to discuss the content of the box.

Many children enjoy the mystery and privacy of such an activity and a parent can only read the content when invited.

This seems to work well for all primary school ages and younger children might just draw pictures.

If the problem is solved, then both of you can comfortably tear up the thought that was written on paper.

Teachers often keep mystery boxes in their class with all sorts of ideas and suggestions to use over the year. It's all about the mystery of the box!

What number are you?

An easy way to get a measure of how children feel – angry, irritable, moody – is to simply ask them to give you a number between one to ten, which is a strategy that I've mentioned throughout this book. Ten is the strongest feeling and one is the lowest. This is about recognising emotions on a scale and it's a common tool used in counselling.

Once parents get into asking children, 'On a scale of one to ten how are you feeling today?', children easily understand the strength of their feelings.

This is helpful in getting a quick measure of how deep the feeling is. It also works well for positive feelings, for example:

> 'You're happy today. On a scale on one to ten,
> how happy are you?'

Classrooms often contain posters with scales and measurements on them. Children learn that a quick response is often easier than long explanations of how they're feeling. This gets the message across to the teacher. It's sometimes the case that a child isn't ready to give long explanations of their feelings and they may need time to process their thoughts. This is especially the case with younger children who are still learning the art of conversation.

Chapter 27

Strategies to manage anxiety

How to talk to children when they feel anxious

There are no absolute answers here but there are smart ways to engage with your child when you detect their feelings of being uncertain about something.

Often, the underlying feeling they have is being fearful of not succeeding in some way. This is often through not achieving at school in their work or in their friendships.

It's firstly important to be still and listen to what they have to say. This means not asking tricky questions; imagine if it was *your* anxieties that were being questioned. We all feel vulnerable and people asking us questions can often get irritating and shut us down. Children feel exactly the same way and they can shut down on us quickly if they feel they're being judged.

Listening to the whole story and offering reinforcements of their feelings can be helpful. For example:

'It sounds like that was difficult.'

'You must be feeling unhappy about that.'

We hear their feeling and wait for them to talk it through. Sometimes we need to allow plenty of time for them to respond.

I find, when working with children, this helps them to simply think through their problems. They're more inclined to chat to parents about their concerns if they feel that their parents will not automatically offer a solution.

Remember, as a parent, *the problem isn't ours to solve*. Once we solve it for them, we have taken over the problem and this isn't great for building resilience in our children.

How to help your child cope

Do you often wonder if you're helping your child effectively cope with all the pressures and stresses that come their way as they grow?

Helping your child cope isn't about taking over their problems and it's also not about giving them solutions that you think would solve their problems. By doing this, they've become your problems! In fact, helping your child is more about having a supportive presence in their world to suit the occasion.

Being in a strong and trusting relationship with your child puts you in a comfortable situation to be invited into their problems. Your child is more inclined to talk about their issues if they feel that you'll listen with compassion and understanding. They don't expect an immediate response or reactionary behaviour. Instead, they expect a calm listener who wants to hear all about their problems and feel their pain. Once your child feels comfortable in talking to you about their concerns, you can ease into asking some details to clarify how they feel. For example:

> *'You seem upset that Mark pushed you in the yard and you don't know what to do because he's your friend.'*

Here, you're playing back their concerns with interest.

Once you have a clear understanding you can seek their approval to make some suggestions. For example:

> *'I'm sure you have your own ideas, but would you like me to suggest some ideas to help solve this problem?'*

Here you can discuss optional ways to address the concern together. The key factor is to be invited into discussing the problem as a guest. In this way, your child is in control of their own problem and is more inclined to solve it themselves.

Operating this way with your child is about maintaining a safe zone. You're not interfering with your child's right to own their problem and they'll get the rewards from solving it themselves. You're merely giving some consultation.

After they've made attempts to work though their problem, you can inquire how it all went and affirm their decisions. If it's still unresolved, you can use the same process to work on helping with further solutions. Think about your own dilemmas at work; no one enjoys others taking control of your own issues.

This concept of giving your child their right to respond to problems should start at an early age. The more we delay their ability to feel in control, the harder it is for them to be sole operators of their own emotions. Success comes from being mentally in charge of themselves.

When working with children who were experiencing concerns with friends at school, it was common practice to invite them to come up with optional ways to deal with the issue. I would make suggestions when invited and later check in to see how they went with solving the problem. If a resolution wasn't reached, it became an exercise in learning about how friends move on and how you understand young friendships. Children learn from the journey of dealing with their own problems and success comes from knowing that they were in charge throughout the entire exercise.

'Whatever happens, take responsibility.'
– Tony Robbins

What's really the truth for a child?

Let's refer to our younger children, pre-schoolers and possibly up to ten years old. A concerned parent sometimes has difficulty in finding the truth from tricky situations that usually end up in tears.

When a child is under pressure and feels some anxiety in explaining a situation which could lead them into trouble and no doubt prove their guilt, it's not uncommon that they can fantasise situations to avoid the truth. To me, this isn't actually lying but it is about a child's mind finding a coping mechanism to ensure that their anxieties stop rising. This is sometimes hard for parents to accept, especially if the truth is very obvious. Sometimes, with older children, they will focus on the blame and shaming of others involved or those that caused them to do the wrong thing. This was common with school squabbles. This is displacement: another way of coping by not telling the truth and reducing their anxiety levels.

Of course, a vicious cycle can then switch into action. Parents become angrier and more frustrated and so their child will hold onto their fantasy to save their emotional state. Sometimes they simply become silent, which further frustrates parents.

Let's look at this another way. If we want the truth, we need to set up an environment that not only encourages the truth, but also affirms and celebrates the child's ability to speak the truth.

Here are some strategies that families can use to encourage children – especially younger ones – to tell the truth:

- When a child tells the truth, even over incidental and less emotive reasons, affirm them. For example:

*'Thanks for telling the truth about the spilt milk.
I know that you understand how slippery and
dangerous it can be on the floor.'*

Here you recognise that telling the truth improved the situation.

- As a family, talk about how telling the truth is important to you. Talk about people you know and value that always tell the truth. Are they well respected?

- Sometimes children's movies have themes of telling the truth. If watching one, highlight the advantages in speaking the truth.

- When an incident occurs, watch your body language. If you appear hostile and anxious to know the truth, you might not get it as emotional barriers quickly rise in your child. Talk about a time – perhaps as a child yourself – where you found it difficult to tell the truth. How did you feel afterwards when it was all over?

When the truth is given, remember that both forgiveness and moving on are very important. Your unconditional love for your child is clear when you can move on from the problem, especially when they've been truthful.

When working with children, especially those that were sent to me for some unacceptable behaviour, I would begin by saying:

> *'I'm hoping that you can help me find out about the incident as I need to help everyone concerned.'*

This is being proactive. It then puts the child in a less vulnerable situation and shifts the guilt to the centre of the problem. Once the child admitted their involvement, it's a matter of thanking them for their honesty before dealing with the overall problem. This comfortably led them to be honest. The less anxious the child felt, the better the outcome in finding the truth.

Lastly, maintaining a child's dignity is important throughout this whole exercise.

The power of walking away

Here I would like to remind you of an excellent strategy and one that's used by many people when they feel overwhelmed. This strategy works on various levels. It's all about the art of walking away when everything gets too much. This strategy works because it creates some emotional space between the incident and the feelings of heightened anger or frustration which invariably lead to an explosion.

Does this look like you at times?

Once you leave the immediacy of a situation and simply distance yourself from what has upset you, you'll automatically slow this heightened feeling down. Other forms of this strategy are to avoid walking into situations when you know you'll react. This is taking a proactive stand.

Creating distance has a remarkable calming effect on the intensity of a problem. If the problem was a ten out of ten, now it might be an eight out of ten.

If you anticipate reacting badly to some potential situation at home, can you remove yourself for a short period to slow down your response? It really works.

Removing yourself is effective for the following reasons:

- You won't overreact or say and do things that you might later regret. Keeping everything in proportion is important.

- Creating space helps you have time to process a problem and put it into perspective. It's amazing how your brain works to recover from the heightened anger when you allow mental space.
- It allows children to think about what's just happened and this gives them time to respond with less anxiety.
- You'll generally sound calmer and direct your comments to your child in a more acceptable way. They're more likely to listen if you're in control.
- The more you train yourself to step away when feeling upset, the more you'll appreciate that the outcomes are better for all concerned.
- You're also demonstrating to your child that you need time to understand what's just occurred.

Keep in mind you need to manage how you communicate with your child by being in control. When situations look precarious, find ways to step away from the situation – at least for a little while until you feel more in control. While living around each other in confined spaces, train yourself to recognise the trigger signs that set you off. Being in control will also be noticed by your children which is a reassuring agent for them.

Practise walking away in your mind and perhaps physically walking away from the situation for a moment. Be silent in voice and body. You have nothing to lose but much to gain in showing effective self-discipline in highly charged situations.

'The best answer to anger is silence.'
– Marcus Aurelius

How to get rid of that blue feeling

It's hard to keep a positive mood all the time, even with children. They get quite crowded with thoughts and desires and sometimes struggle to put order into their life.

It's not uncommon to find a child feeling and looking quite idle and down in the day. When this occurs, there is a simple and easy way to lift that spirit and, most importantly, to give your child strategies to help them control their moods. Remember what you're doing here is teaching your child how to manage their moods better.

Suggest that they write a list of activities or things that makes them feel happy. This could include everything from Lego, to dolls, to playing games, seeing friends and so on. The point of this exercise is to discuss the list of suggestions that can very quickly shift a mood or temperament.

Put the list somewhere visible and discuss the possibility of engaging in some of these activities or simply discussing the fun and joy they receive from them. The purpose of this exercise is to give the child a way out of thinking moody thoughts. It's about redirecting them to the positive and distracting their negative feelings. Keep the list visible for a while and suggest that the list should be upgraded from time to time, especially when new experiences come into play.

When working with children, it was common practice that they would write down activities or resources that made them feel good. It acted as a distraction from sad feelings and it also proved an excellent vehicle to talk about what was valuable in their life. Classrooms would be set up for free time where children worked on their own projects for enjoyment.

Children generally like to write or draw their feelings and it's not an uncommon way to express themselves. A younger child without writing skills can simply draw the things that make them feel happy.

You can also model this behaviour to your child by keeping your own list. This is a great example to them that you use similar strategies to deal with mood swings.

A little bit of distraction can go a long way to redirecting feelings.

> *'Start writing no matter what.*
> *The water does not flow until the faucet is turned on.'*
> **– Louis L'Amour**

Laughter a great tool in dealing with stress and anxiety

How often do you laugh with your children? Do you find the things they do or talk about amusing? Can you see the lighter side of your child's actions when you remember that they're the actions of a child and not an adult?

Our world can easily be seen as a serious place and children have a natural disposition to be happy and seek out happy spaces and people. In fact, they're a delight to be with and a privilege to have in our lives.

Laughing with your child is a healthy activity to do. It also teaches your child that humour is valued and that finding humour in life situations can be very mentally therapeutic. Some people have a natural disposition to see the world in lighter ways. For others, finding the lighter side to life can be learnt overtime.

We can all see situations through different perspectives; is the glass half full or empty? Finding the funny side to situations is an excellent way to teach your child a strategy in coping with stress.

As previously mentioned, children are attracted to warmth in personality and humour and, as a parent, we can sometimes become absorbed in the seriousness of the occasion. After all, our role is to rear our children and to provide for them. However, it's also a parent's role to teach their children strategies that enable them to cope better when times are difficult. It's also about showing them that there's humour and lightness when sometimes everything seems out of control.

Teachers are very clever at selecting moments in class that bring spontaneous laughter to the classroom. This creates a climate in the room which is inviting and optimistic. It says to the children, 'We're a happy class. Mistakes happen and we move on while only seeing the brighter side of the day.' It's a wonderful way of taking away built-up tension.

When working with children individually, I would start the conversation on a positive note and try to bring in something light and happy to talk about. If we both enjoyed a joke, it created the environment for more comfortable talk to follow.

Laughing about yourself teaches your child that you're a resilient person.

Of course, it's important to recognise a serious situation.

But let's look at the advantages of bringing humour into your family life:

- It costs nothing.

- It enlivens the spirit.
- It gives a strong message to your child that humour is an important aspect in your life.
- It lightens anxiety.
- It invites your child to read a situation for what it is rather than becoming too serious.
- It reminds your child that the world isn't a perfect place, and that perfection can be restrictive.
- If your child is laughing at you it teaches them that you're resilient when people find you funny.
- It also helps a child discern what is serious and what is acceptable humour. For some children, this can take some time to understand.

Laughter is life giving. It's a wonderful collective activity to do as a family and it strengthens aspects of self-esteem and self-worth.

'A day without laughter is a day wasted.'
– Charlie Chaplin

Afterword

This book offers support to families who are about to embrace or are somewhere on the journey of primary school education. The content is born from my belief that a school can have a major impact on the social, emotional, intellectual and physical growth of a child. There are many ups and downs with children and their families throughout their life in primary school and I've included some insights into how children can be supported during this time. These insights come from my own experience in working with children and supporting families by facilitating parent education courses, studying counselling and experiencing thirty-nine years in education – ten as a teacher and twenty-nine as a principal.

There is no doubt that school experiences influence a child's development. At the primary level, a child's growth is immense, and this book gives suggestions and reflections on how that journey can be made more successful and, above all, a happy experience for everyone in the family. School is a powerful tool in shaping a child's vision of the world and themselves. I hope the suggestions and reflections I offered provides some enlightenment and guidance as your child weaves their way through their primary years.

About the author

Gail Smith was born in Melbourne and completed her secondary education at Catholic Ladies College. She went on to achieve a Master of Educational Leadership (ACU) and a Master of Counselling (ACU), Graduate Diploma in Urban Sociology (Swinburne). Gail is a marriage celebrant and was an accredited Parent Effectiveness Trainer and Growth Coach. A mother of three and a grandmother of five, Gail was a teacher at three schools – and Principal at three other Primary Schools.

Since retirement she has published the website blog that can be found at www.theprimaryyears.com

Index

A

access versus ownership, 157–60
accountability, 171–2, *see also* blame
achievement, 101–2, 109–11, 241, *see also* capabilities; goal-setting; problem-solving; success
affection, 111, 221–2, 252
 unconditional love, 102, 113, 221–2, 355
 see also parent-child attachment
affirmation, 81, 88, 94–6, 101–2, 103, 134–5
 of achievement, 101–2, 109–11
 child modelling of, 110–11
 in development of self-awareness, 69–70
 in effective listening, 131–2
 of effort (having a go), 71, 101–2, 289
 of failure as part of success, 98–100
 of finishing a task, 177–9
 of helpfulness, 79–80
 of independence, 152–4
 in managing attention-seeking, 191–3
 of negotiation, 234, 258
 of others, 244–6
 of perseverance, 77, 99, 154–6
 in problem-solving, 77–8, 99, 286, 332, 352
 in risk-taking, 149–50
 showing confidence in children, 70–2
 of truth-telling, 354
 see also praise

anger in children, 137, 147–8, 340–1, *see also* conflict
anger in parents, 250–1, 252
 walking away technique, 334, 356–7
anxiety in children
 boundaries and, 58 *see also* routine and structure
 coping with early stress at school, 271–8
 dealing with, 325–30
 as emotional blocker, 46
 fear of making mistakes, 170, 288–9
 happy thoughts focus, 248–9
 learning environment and lesson breaks, 143
 from overthinking, 168–70
 parents and, 325–37
 practical activities to reduce anxiety, 339–48
 practical strategies to manage anxiety, 350–61
 schoolwork, 101, 286–8, 326
 sibling behaviour, 236–8
 sources of, 314–23, 325–8
 upset children, 128–30
 see also happiness; school fatigue; trauma
apologising, 66–8, 113, 334, *see also* mistakes
attachment *see* parent-child attachment
attention span, 26–7
attention-giving by parents, 130–2, *see also* listening

attention-seeking behaviour, 191–3, 235–8
authority, 309, 330–1
Autism Spectrum Disorder (ASD), 235, 341

B

bad days, 246–7, 344, 358–9, *see also* emotions
balanced life, 4–5, 269–70
bedtime, 58–9, 62–4, 206
behaviour (children), 86–105
   attention-seeking, 191–3, 235–8
   behaviour change and school absences, 303–5
   change motivation, 86–9
   coaching by parents, 89–91
   difficult and demanding, 235–8
   goal-setting, 91, 100–2
   parental expectations and reassurance, 94–6, 249–50
   poor behaviour, dealing with, 92–4, 102–5, 112, 126, 253–5
   resilience-building, 96–7
   see also anger in children; anxiety in children; emotions
behaviour of others, 156–7
bias *see* discrimination
birthdays
   lesson in patience, 159, 176
   parties, 191, 284
   treats, 240
blame, 97, 116, 190, 328–9, 354
   versus building, 170–2
   see also judgemental attitudes, avoidance of
body image, 322–3
body language, 18–20, 51, 193
   facial expressions, 104, 216, 333–4
boredom, 60
boundaries, 57–9, 112–13, 209–12, *see also* routine and structure
budgeting, 158–60

C

calmness, 40, 52, 93, 97, 102–3, 129, 136, 189–90, 193, 194–5, *see also* anger in children; anger in parents; upset children; upset parents
capabilities
   doubts about, 335–7
   recognition of, 20–3, 151–4
   see also self-esteem
celebrations of national days, 118–20
charts, 146–7, 276–7, 342
child development, 13–14, 315
child modelling of affirmation, 110–11
childcare, 268–70
children
   behaviour of *see* behaviour
   capabilities, 20–3, 151–4
   conversing with *see* conversations with children
   doubts about abilities, 335–7
   emotional strengths, 21
   facial expressions, 104, 216, 333–4
   information processing, 27–8, 52–4, 168–70
   life skills, 21–2
   mindset, 164–8
   opinions, 41–2, 47–9, 188
   order in family, 233, 240
   parent-child attachment, 206–7, 221–3
   quiet children, 241, 314–17
   self-awareness, 68–70
   self-confidence *see* confidence development
   self-esteem, 11–12, 283
   sense of justice, 72–3
   sense of time, 217
   siblings *see* siblings
   upset children, 128–32, 156–7, 329–30
children's books, 321, 345–6, *see also* reading

Index

child's name, use in conversation, 39, 51
coaching, 89–91, *see also* instructions
collaboration *see* cooperation
comfort zone, departure from *see* new experiences
compassion, 189–91
computers *see* technology
confidence development
    doubts about abilities, 335–7
    giving children a voice, 47–9, 193, 239, 315–17 *see also* conversations with children
    showing parental confidence, 70–2
confidentiality of information in a school setting, 296
conflict
    defending oneself, 156–7
    recognition and management, 135–7
    between siblings, 82, 157, 233–5, 239
    see also anger in children
consistency, 257–8, 262–3
control *see* power relationships
control of emotions *see* emotions
conversations with children
    acknowledging child capabilities, 20–3
    anxiety management *see* anxiety in children
    attention-giving by parents, 130–2
    body language, 18–20, 51
    child information processing, 27–8, 45–7, 52–4
    dealing with poor behaviour, 92–4, 102–5
    explanations (parental techniques), 26–9, 330–3
    honesty in, 228–31, 262
    managing attention-seeking behaviour, 192–3
    'no' response, 43, 159
    opportunities for, 205–6
    parenting style and, 107–9, 262–3
    presenting virtues and values, 189–90
    questioning techniques, 43–4, 113–16
    timing, 27–8, 42–5, 102–3, 130, 131, 321
    upset children, 129
    see also instructions; listening; parenting
cooperation, 78, 190, 197–9, 308, *see also* helpfulness
coping skills *see* problem-solving
counsellors and counselling, 145–6, 191, 237, 320, 347
creative activities, 160–2, 168, 216, 217, 219
crisis *see* family crisis
criticism, subtle, avoidance of, 71
cultural and linguistic differences, 201–3
curiosity *see* knowledge; learning
cyber safety, 308–9

D

death, 229, 317, 326–7
decision-making, 321
    coaching in, 89–91
differences
    in family operation, 257–8
    in parenting style, 107–9, 261–3
    in siblings, 238–42
    in society, 201–3, 258–61
different experiences *see* new experiences
discrimination, 258–61
divorce *see* family separation
doubts about abilities, 335–7
downtime, 60–2
drama (acting out situations), 219, 344–5
drawing, 125, 216, 219, 341–2, 358–9

E

eating between meals, 58, 59
education
    changes in, 9–10
    see also childcare; pre-school; school; teachers
effort (having a go), 71, 101–2, 170, 289, *see also* perseverance
emotions
    bad days, 246–7, 344, 358–9
    books for reading about feelings, 345–6
    expression of, 147–8, 156–7, 250–2, 358–9
    parents' negative emotions, 250–1, 252
    parents' negative thoughts about children, 253–5
    parents' regulation of own mood swings, 333–5, 359
    talking about feelings, 21, 147–8, 156, 275, 329–30, 342–3, 347–8
    see also anxiety in children; happiness
empathy, 189–91
encouragement, 71–2, *see also* affirmation
enjoying the moment, 122–6
explanations *see* conversations with children

F

facial expressions, 104, 216, *see also* body language
failure, learning from, 98–100, 164–6, 288–9, *see also* success
familiarity *see* new experiences; routine and structure
families
    changing nature of, 186–8
    different ways of operating, 257–8
    see also children; parents; siblings
family activities, 116–20, 158, 189–91, 192–3, 222, 239
    breaks, 142–3
    planning for time together, 225–8
    right time for, 141–2
    rituals in family life, 208–9
    see also home environment; play
family budget, 158–60
family crisis, 57–8, 97, 186–8
family meetings, 63, 237, 299, 329–30
family relationship with school, 6–9, 270–3, 290–1, 293–6
family separation, 229, 317–22, 329, *see also* trauma
family stories, 69–70, 159, 203
fantasising, 353–6, *see also* honesty
fatigue *see* school fatigue; tired children; tired parents
feelings *see* emotions
finishing *see* perseverance
fixed mindset, 164–8
flexibility *see* variety and flexibility
free time *see* downtime
friendship, 202
    making friends, 143–5, 273–6, 282–5
    problems, 77, 285–6, 353
    see also social life

G

gifts (strengths) *see* capabilities
goal-setting, 91, 100–2, 146–7, 155–6, 336–7
gossip, 294–5
gratitude, 189–91
growth mindset, 164–8

H

happiness, 13, 217, 222, 247–52, 358–9, *see also* laughter
happy journal, 145–6
'having a go' *see* effort (having a go)
help, asking for, 138–41
helpfulness, 78–80
holidays, 59, 299–300, 308
home environment, 117, 212–13

consistent rules, 257–8
creative space, 161–2
homework, 58, 139–40, 294, 305–6, 307, *see also* schoolwork
honesty, 66–8, 69, 111, 171–2, 228–31, 262, 320
   affirmation of, 354
   telling the truth, 353–6

I
images, 12–13
imaginative play *see* drama (acting out situations); play
independence
   affirmation of, 152–4
   development of, 151–4, 207, 221–2, 291
information processing, 27–8, 52–4, 168–70
instructions
   child processing of, 52–4
   parental strategies, 49–52
   see also coaching; conversations with children

J
jokes, 252, 360
journals, 145–6, 227
judgemental attitudes, avoidance of, 111, 179–81, 194, 261–2, *see also* blame; opinions
justice, sense of, 72–3

K
kindergarten, 268–70
kindness, 189–91
knowledge, 172–4, *see also* learning

L
language
   effective, 38–40
   explanations (techniques), 26–9
   expression of feelings, 147–8, 156–7
   incidental, 36–8
   negative, 31, 34–7, 47, 71–2
   positive, 31, 32–4, 40, 97
   power of words, 29–31, 40
   in talking about issues, 45–7
language development, 268–70, 309
laughter, 124, 216, 249, 359–61, *see also* happiness
learning, 172–4, 198–203, 270–1, 303–4
   from children, 215–19
   inquiry-based approach, 138–41
   interest in, 10, 173–4
   lesson breaks, 142–3
   literacy and numeracy, 5–6, 269
   from mistakes and failure, 98–100, 164–6, 288–9
   teacher's role, 10–11, 172–3, 197
   see also knowledge; school; teachers
life balance, 4–5, 269–70
limits *see* boundaries
listening, 50–2, 72–3, 107–8, 111
   active listening, 192–3
   effective listening, 130–2, 189–90, 194–5
   see also conversations with children
love, unconditional, 113, 221–2, 355, *see also* parent-child attachment

M
media *see* social media; television
memories, 124–5
mindfulness, 122–6
mindset, 164–8
mistakes
   child learning from, 98–100, 164–6, 288–9
   parental acknowledgement of, 66–8, 113, 334
   see also success

N
name use in conversations, 39, 51
narrative therapy, 145–6
national celebrations, 118–20

negative behaviour *see* poor behaviour, dealing with
negative feelings
  in children, 358–9
  parental display of negative emotions, 250–1, 252
  by parents about children, 102–4, 253–5
negative language, 31, 34–6, 47, 71–2
  gossip, 294–5
negotiation, 51–2, 72–3, 112, 136, 224–5, 258
  affirmation of, 234, 258
new experiences, 148–51, 167–8, 201–3
'no' response, interpretation of, 43, 159

O

older people, 200, 201–2, 326–7
one-on-one time, 117, 122–6, 194–5, 236–7, 238, 239–40
open mindset *see* growth mindset
opinions
  avoidance of judgemental attitudes, 111, 179–81, 194, 261–2
  child expression of, 41–2, 47–9, 188
  parent expression of, 41–2, 179–81
  see also blame
outdoor activities, 61, 83, 161–2, 218, 219, 308
overthinking, 168–70, *see also* information processing
ownership versus access, 157–60

P

parent-child attachment, 206–7, 221–3, *see also* affection; independence
parenting, 23–6, 107–20
  authority, 309, 330–1
  effectiveness, 111–13
  giving praise, 109–11
  helping your child cope, 351–61
  practical activities to reduce anxiety, 339–48
  practical strategies to manage anxiety, 327–8, 350–61
  styles, 107–9, 261–3
  tips for school starting, 274–8
  tips for supporting children at school, 290–1
  tips to make life easier, 116–18
  virtues and values, 189–91
  see also anxiety in children; conversations with children; routine and structure
parents
  acknowledgement of mistakes, 66–8, 113, 334
  being childlike, 217–19
  and children's anxiety, 325–37
  as early educators, 270–1
  fatigue, 83, 228, 334
  mindset, 166–8
  mood swings and their regulation, 333–5, 359
  negative emotions display, 250–1, 252
  negative feelings about children, 102–4, 253–5
  opinions, 41–2, 179–81
  personal space, 206–7
  as role models, 66–73, 76, 96–7, 110–11, 307, 309–10
  self-discipline, 356–7
  separation, 229, 317–22
patience, 175–7, 192–3
perseverance, 77, 99, 154–6, 177–9
personal space (parents), 206–7
personal time (children) *see* downtime
personal worth *see* self-esteem
pets, 59
phones *see* technology
play, 216, 218–19, 239
  cooperative play, 135
  outdoor activities, 61, 83, 161–2, 218, 219, 308

Index

play dates, 202
see also family activities; sport
pocket money, 159
poor behaviour, dealing with, 92–4, 102–5, 112, 126, 253–5
positive language, 31, 32–4, 40, 97
positive psychology, 145–6
positivity, 13, 244–55
   about school starting, 274–8
   in school environment, 294–5
   see also happiness
power relationships, 223–5, 330–3
praise, 109–11, 134–5, 189, *see also* affirmation
predictability *see* routine and structure
prejudice *see* discrimination
pre-school, 268–70
pride, 84, 94–5
primary education *see* learning; school
proactivity, 80–4, 171
problem-solving, 153–4
   affirmation in, 77–8, 99, 286, 332, 352
   building versus blaming, 170–2
   helping your child cope, 351–61
   modelling resolution of problems, 96–7
   practical activities, 339–48, 358–9
   questions and tips, 76–7
   resilience and, 96–7
   value of, 75–8
   see also anxiety in children

Q

questioning
   asking for help, 138–41
   techniques, 43–4, 113–16
   timing, 43–5
   see also conversations with children
quiet children, 241, 314–17

R

reading, 5–6, 189, 208, 269, 309–10, 317, 327
   in bed, 58, 63
   cessation after trauma, 318
   to children, 117, 198
   with children, 309–10
   stories with a message, 345–6
reassurance, 94–6, 249–50, 319–20
resilience, 11, 96–7
restorative practice, 72–3
reward systems
   'having a go' sheets, 189
   notes to children, 22, 70, 104–5, 249–50
   sticker charts, 146–7
   success charts, 276–7
risk-taking, 149–50, *see also* new experiences
rituals in family life, 208–9
role models, 66–73, 76, 96–7, 110–11, 307, 309–10
routine and structure, 56–9, 149
   bedtime, 62–4
   boundaries, 57–9, 112–13, 209–12
   consistent rules, 257–8
   school, 275, 276–7, 298–301, 303

S

sad feelings *see* anxiety in children; emotions
sandpits/sand trays, 340–1
school, 280–91
   attendance consistency, 303–5
   confidentiality of information, 296
   family relationship with, 6–9, 270–3, 290–1, 293–6
   friendships at, 273–4, 282–5 *see also* friendship
   pre-school, 269–70
   reluctance to attend, 285–6, 304–5
   return after holidays, 299–300

routine, 275, 276–7, 298–301, 303
starting school, 269–78
supporting children at school, 290–1
tests, 286–8, 326
see also learning; teachers
school communities, 294–6, 300–1
school fatigue, 280–2
school office team, 300–1
school refusal, 285–6, 304–5
school year, 298–301
schoolwork
    anxiety about, 101, 288–9, 326
    display at home, 271, 277
    homework, 58, 139–40, 294, 305–6, 307
self-awareness, 68–70
self-confidence *see* confidence development
self-esteem, 11–12, 283, *see also* capabilities
self-regard, 143–5
sensitivity, 329–30
separation *see* family separation
sharing, 135, 190, 192, 197–8, *see also* cooperation
siblings, 96
    conflict, 82, 157, 233–5, 239
    cooperation, 197–8
    differences, 238–42
    order of, 233, 240
silence, 28, 32, 46, 193, 315–17
sleep, 62–4, 290
social development, 268–70
social life, 190–1, *see also* friendship
social media, 142, 181
    body image and, 323
    monitoring by parents, 175, 309
society
    cultural and linguistic differences, 201–3
    differences and discrimination, 258–61
sport, 4, 21, 155, 198–9, 228, 244, 322–3, 325–6
staying power *see* perseverance
sticker charts, 146–7
structure *see* routine and structure
'stupid' (term), 31, 35–6
success, 4–5
    achievement, 101–2, 109–11, 241
    affirmation of others' success, 244–6
    learning from mistakes, 98–100, 164–6, 288–9
    school tests, 286–8
    see also mistakes
success charts, 276–7
supportive behaviour in parents, 128–32

T

talking about feelings *see* emotions
talking with children *see* conversations with children; instructions; listening
tasks
    completion of, 177–9
    instructions and negotiation, 50–2
    see also perseverance
teachers
    confidentiality and, 296
    importance of, 10–11, 272–3
    prep teachers, 272–3
    role of, 172–3, 197, 273–4, 285–6, 291
    setting limits, 211–12
    see also school
teamwork *see* cooperation
technology, 257, 258, 306–9
television, 61, 257, 306–9
temper *see* anger in children; anger in parents
time, sense of, 217
timing

in dealing with issues, 42–5, 102–3, 130, 131
of discussion of family separation, 321
of explanations, 27–8
right time for activities, 141–2
tired children, 43, 62–3, 81–2, 88, 93, 114, 246–7, 277, *see also* school fatigue
tired parents, 83, 228, 334
tone of voice, 19, 27–8, 39–40, 58, 169, 252
toys, 61, 90, 113
trauma, 229, 317–19, *see also* anxiety in children
truth *see* honesty
trying (having a go) *see* effort (having a go)

U

unconditional love, 102, 113, 221–2, 355, *see also* parent-child attachment
upset children, 128–32, 156–7, 329–30, *see also* anger in children
upset parents, 129–30, *see also* anger in parents

V

value
of feeling proud, 84, 94–5
of helping others, 78–80
of proactivity, 80–4
of problem-solving, 75–8
variety and flexibility, 57, 59
virtues and values, 189–91
voice, tone of, 19, 27–8, 39–40, 58, 169, 252

W

walking away technique for managing emotions, 334, 356–7
winning *see* power relationships; success
words *see* language

worries *see* anxiety in children
writing
about happy activities, 358–9
about problems (problem disposal), 343
diaries, 227
literacy, 5–6, 269
notes to children, 22, 70, 104–5, 249–50
stories, 317

www.ingramcontent.com/pod-product-compliance
Lightning Source LLC
Chambersburg PA
CBHW071554080526
44588CB00010B/911